In his long life, W. E. B. Du Bois traveled far and thought deeply about his people. In his search for the meaning of the black experience, he wrote and organized, giving black consciousness one of its earliest contributions in his *The Souls of Black Folk*, taking part in the primary stages of the civil rights movement, and giving voice to the Negro writer in the journal *Crisis*. *Cheer the Lonesome Traveler* is the study of one life which affected change in the lives and thoughts of many.

Leslie Lacy spent some time in Ghana as a university instructor. It is there that he became acquainted with Dr. Du Bois. He is now an assistant professor of African Studies at Howard University and a lecturer in the Albert Schweitzer Program at New York University.

THE LAUREL-LEAF LIBRARY brings together under a single imprint outstanding works of fiction and nonfiction particularly suitable for young adult readers, both in and out of the classroom. This series is under the editorship of M. Jerry Weiss, Distinguished Professor of Communications, Jersey City State College, and Charles F. Reasoner, Professor of Elementary Education, New York University. Dell's special consultant in the social studies is Jane Greenspan, Hunter College High School.

CHEER THE LONESOME TRAVELER

The Life of
W. E. B. Du Bois

by Leslie Alexander Lacy

ILLUSTRATED BY JAMES BARKLEY

Published by
Dell Publishing Co., Inc.
750 Third Avenue
New York, New York 10017

Laurel-Leaf Library ® TM766734, Dell Publishing Co., Inc.
Reprinted by arrangement with The Dial Press,
New York, New York.
Printed in the United States of America
First Laurel printing—January 1972

*Grateful acknowledgment is made for permission to reprint the
following material:*

The Fire Next Time by James Baldwin. Copyright © 1963, 1962 by
James Baldwin. Used by permission of the publisher, The Dial Press.

Excerpts from *Crisis III and IV:* Reprinted from *The Crisis* with the
permission of The Crisis Publishing Company.

First stanza of "Heritage" by Countee Cullen: From *On These I Stand*
by Countee Cullen, Harper & Row, 1947.

"Yet Do I Marvel" by Countee Cullen: From *On These I Stand* by
Countee Cullen. Copyright 1925 by Harper & Brothers. Renewed 1953
by Ida M. Cullen. Reprinted by permission of Harper & Row, Publishers.

The poems beginning with the words "In your presence" ("Auprès de
toi") and "In those days" ("Les vautours") by David Diop were first
published in *Coup de Pilon* by *Presence Africaine*, Paris, 1956.

The Autobiography of W. E. B. Du Bois by W. E. B. Du Bois: Reprinted
by permission of International Publishers Co., Inc. Copyright © 1968.

Black Reconstruction by W. E. B. Du Bois: Used by permission of Mrs.
Shirley Graham Du Bois.

Darkwater by W. E. B. Du Bois: Used by permission of Mrs. Shirley
Graham Du Bois. Published by Schocken Books, Inc.

Dusk of Dawn by W. E. B. Du Bois: Used by permission of Harcourt,
Brace & World, Inc.

*For my restless students at Howard
University, who taught me so much about
the world they want to build and live in.
And for Julius Lester. He has the
best qualities of our generation: morality,
intelligence, indifference to a world which
cares so little about him, and the courage
to take a revolutionary stand against that
world for the betterment of our people.
In every sense he is a child of Du Bois.
I stand with him.*

Contents

"How can the American Negro past be used? It is entirely possible that this dishonored past will rise up soon to smite all of us . . . A bill is coming in that I fear America is not prepared to pay. The problem of the twentieth century, wrote W.E.B. Du Bois around sixty years ago, is the problem of the color line. A fearful and delicate problem, which compromises, when it does not corrupt, all the American efforts to build a better world—here, there, or anywhere. It is for this reason that everything white Americans think they believe in must now be reëxamined."

CHEER THE LONESOME TRAVELER

Let us cheer the weary traveler,
Cheer the weary traveler
Let us cheer the weary traveler . . .
A-long the heavenly way . . .
I'll take my gospel trumpet,
An' I'll begin to blow,
An' if my Savior help me
I blow wherever I go
Let us cheer the weary traveler
Let us cheer the weary traveler
A-long the heavenly way.

traditional Negro spiritual

The End of an Era

Early evenings are usually cool in Accra, the capital city of Ghana. The African sun—hot, tropical, constant, everlasting—hides its face behind the still clouds and allows the gentle breeze from the Atlantic Ocean to make the nights pleasant for sleep. By late evening, except on the weekends, which are always festive, the city is quiet. The village people who came that morning to sell their goods and buy goods produced in the modern worlds of Paris, New York, and London have returned to those villages, where they are now asleep, or talking politics, or drumming, preparing for the return in the morning to the city, or singing songs about their way of life. They live in the twentieth century, but their homes are far from its wars and revolutions, far from its commercial civilizations.

There is some night life in the city—a few movie houses, bars, open-air clubs, and a few hotels. But the morning people, peasants from the land, bring the excitement and color and take it with them when they have gotten their daily bread. What remains are a few Europeans, Arab traders who speak one or more West African languages but are hated by the people nevertheless, and the new African: European on one side; a villager on the other; a product of the colonial period but also very much African. He is a child of two worlds. In his business he speaks and lives in a European world. At night with his wife and children he speaks the language his fathers spoke before the white man came. His food is African, his laughter is loud and unrestrained, like an electric bulb piercing his candlelight darkness. He is the master of his house even though the Europeans and Arabs still dominate his newly self-governing state. And like his relatives still working the land he must extinguish his candle early because the demands of the morning come too soon.

On the evening of August 22, 1963, Accra almost lost its tropical cool. Violence and hatred hung over the city like smog. Fifty angry black people representing a much larger group of Afro-Americans living in exile had gathered in front of the American embassy. It was rumored that they were going to burn down the building and beat up the white Americans inside. But the rumors were false. These angry souls, all of whom had come to Kwame Nkrumah's Ghana to escape the vice of American racism, may have wanted to destroy their country's embassy, but that thought had not brought them there. They had come to stage a protest demonstration in sympathy with thousands of other Americans marching on Washington, D.C., that same day.

It was a complex and fascinating group ranging from a Los Angeles plumber who had memorized all of Chairman Mao Tse-tung's thoughts, to a university professor of philosophy, originally from Georgia but now without an American passport, who spoke English with an upper-class London accent. From different social backgrounds and experiences they were in Ghana helping President Nkrumah and his government to build a new, independent African society. They had long stopped believing in nonviolent direct action as a means of eliminating social injustice but felt that the protest in front of the embassy was the least that they could do to show support and solidarity with the soul folks back home. Serious but a little self-conscious they marched around the building carrying their signs and singing old freedom songs.

Suddenly a fast-moving car stopped abruptly at the front of the picket line. Quickly picketers nearest the car broke ranks and ran over to talk with the driver.

In a few minutes other picketers followed until all fifty had encircled the little English sports cars.

Something was wrong! The picketers nearest the driver were sad. One cursed in disgust; another kicked the cement sidewalk. And another one, barely sixteen, broke his picket sign, looked slowly over his shoulder at the American embassy, and shouted, "America, you killed him. I hate you, America, I hate you."

"What's wrong?" asked a little girl of fifteen. She was standing near the back and had not heard the news the driver had brought.

Her mother looked at her, then held her tightly. "The Old Man is gone. Dr. Du Bois has just died."

Soon all fifty knew that William Edward Burghardt Du Bois was dead. They had all known him, of his illness, but did not want to believe. A woman started to sing the Old Man's favorite spiritual, "Let Us Cheer the Weary Traveler." Tension mounted as police piled out of army trucks to protect the extension of America on Ghanaian soil. But they were not needed. Law and order prevailed. Tension subsided. The evening was cool again and the protestors continued their peaceful demonstration.

I was one of those fifty people. This biography began that evening. At first it was just a dramatic thought, a balance to the tragic news. But during the next days, after the state funeral and burial in Osu, I had more thoughts and made many notes. His death made me think of his life.

W. E. B. Du Bois was dead at ninety-five. He had served his beliefs; he had served his fellowman. He had led a varied life as a teacher, sociologist, editor, writer. In 1903 he had told the world in his book *The Souls of Black Folk*, "the problem of the twentieth century is the problem of the color line." Now he was dead, and the problem which he had prophesied was still as real. His keen insight had caused one literary critic, Madeline Stratton, to remark, "The career of W. E. B. Du Bois will reflect a light across the memory of man as long as man seeks and reveres the ideals of justice and liberty, of intelligence and beauty."

Very few Americans understood and believed what this critic said. Again and again Du Bois spoke to America:

One ever feels his
twoness—an American,
a Negro; two souls, two
unreconciled strivings;
two warring ideals in
one dark body, whose
dogged strength alone
keeps it from being
torn asunder. . . .

But most of America did not hear his words. In the country of his birth he was a prophet without honor.

It is my intention to take another look at William Edward Burghardt Du Bois's life. As I began to write, I quickly realized that it was difficult to understand such a great historical figure and perhaps the best way to see Du Bois was by probing some of the lingering questions about his long life. What was the young Du Bois really like? Why was the conflict between him and Booker T. Washington so intense? Why did he criticize Marcus Garvey, the black nationalist of the twenties who advocated a "Back to Africa" plan? What were Du Bois's ideas about a united Africa? After spending most of his life rejecting communism, why did he belatedly join the Communist party? Why did he eventually reject America to become a Ghanaian citizen? And finally how did Du Bois come to view himself?

Primarily this biography is for the young. Du Bois loved young people, especially those who would stand up for truth. In Ghana he said to me, "Every time the young say 'no' another year is added to my life."

I knew W. E. B. Du Bois but a brief moment in Africa. I was not fortunate enough to be always around: helping, listening, absorbing, witnessing a century come to a close. I envy those who were.

But I deeply respected him. Inevitably he is the kind of man you come to love. I loved his wit, his aristocratic smile, his arrogance, his masculinity, and all the questions he was sure to ask you. Deeper, much deeper, I loved the history of his life. I loved his face, brown like the African sand, changing so fast in his last days on earth. Dr. William Edward Burghardt Du Bois, an Afro-American who came from New England, a Harvard scholar, a writer of many books, a teacher, a civil-rights leader, a spokesman for Africa and people of

African descent, a man who lived almost a century, a beautiful human being, died in Africa.

In his blood he had carried his African past and now, the past and present would come together. And his death was not among strangers. The Ghanaians who knew him loved him and sang his praises to the heavens. In a way of speaking you could say that it was the Africans who would finally reach out for his soul and lay it to final rest. Lines from the Ghanaian poet Korbina Parkes capture the feelings of what many Ghanaians felt:

Give me black souls
let them be black
or chocolate brown
or make them the
color of dusk
dustlike,
browner than sand.

LESLIE ALEXANDER LACY

Howard University
1969

Now as I was young and easy under the apple boughs
About the lilting house and happy as the grass was green,
   The night above the dingle starry,
    Time let me hail and climb
    Golden in the heydays of his eyes,
And honoured among wagons I was prince of the apple
  towns
And once below a time I lordly had the trees and leaves
     Trail with daisies and barley
    Down the rivers of the windfall light.

DYLAN THOMAS

The Making of a Prophet

There is a town in the southwestern corner of Massachusetts called Great Barrington. Twenty-eight miles from the Hudson River, bounded on the west by New York State and on the south by Connecticut, it is the business center of the southern Berkshire towns. It is famous for its mountains, streams, lakes, riding trails, and those delightfully shaded back roads where you can roam or ride at will. Like most southern Berkshire towns, Great Barrington is small. Settled in 1726, its population has never been more than seven thousand. It has two newspapers, *The Berkshire Courier*, published weekly in Great Barrington, and *The Berkshire Eagle*, published daily in a little town called Pittsfield. There is one radio station that plays good hillbilly music and a small modern motion picture theater with first-run films. Besides this Great Barrington is near the Berkshire Symphonic Festival at Tanglewood; the Sunday evening Berkshire Music Barn at Lenox; and the Dance Festival at Jacobs Pillow.

William Edward Burghardt Du Bois was born in this New England village. Naturally it has changed since his time, but the changes are few—more like fixing up an old car rather than getting a new one. The description of Great Barrington that Du Bois wrote fifty years ago is still very much true today: "My town was shut in by its mountains and provincialism; but it was a beautiful place . . . nestled shyly in its valley with something of Dutch cleanliness and English reticence. . . ."

In fact if you leave South Main Street and ride Route 23 to the edge of the community, you can stand on the ground where Du Bois was born. The farmhouse where he lived as a child is gone, but the site has been proclaimed a national memorial.

In his now famous autobiography, *Dusk of Dawn*, Du Bois tells us, "I was born by a golden river and in the shadow of two great hills. . . . The house . . . was quaint, with clapboards running up and down, neatly trimmed, and there were five rooms, a tiny porch, a rosy front yard, and unbelievably delicious strawberries in the rear. . . ."

But the era in which he was born was more important than the place of his birth. Willie, as the young Du Bois was called, was a child of the Civil War. He was born on February 23, 1868, one day after George Washington's birthday and three years after the North had defeated the South. He would live in a divided America.

On the surface of the land there was talk of peace, unity, freedom, and brotherhood. Slavery had been abolished and the Fifteenth Amendment had further assured these sons and daughters of Africa that law and justice would prevail. A new day was coming. Black men, some barely literate, voted new constitutions all over the South. Union troops were stationed throughout the ex-Confederacy to make very sure that this new freedom and reconstruction would yield progress for all. Much later Du Bois, in *Black Reconstruction in America, 1860–1880,* describes the then prevailing mood in black America:

Suppose on some gray day, as you plod down Wall Street, you should see God sitting on the Treasury steps, in His Glory, with the thunders curved about him? Suppose on Michigan Avenue, between the lakes and hills of stone, and in the midst of hastening automobiles and jostling crowds, suddenly you see living and walking towards you, the Christ, with sorrow and sunshine in his face?

Foolish talk, all of this, you say, of course; and that is because no American now believes in his religion. . . . But to most of the four million black folk emancipated by the civil war, God was real. They knew him. They had met him personally in many a wild orgy of religious frenzy, or in the black stillness of night. His plan for them was clear; they were to suffer and be degraded, and then afterwards by Divine edict, raised to manhood and power; and so on January 1, 1863, He made them free.

It was all foolish, bizarre, and tawdry. Gangs of dirty Negroes howling and dancing; poverty-stricken ignorant laborers mistaking war, destruction, and revolution for the mystery of the free human soul; and yet to these black folk it was the Apocalypse. The magnificent trumpet tones of Hebrew Scripture, transmuted and oddly changed, became a strange new gospel. All that was Beauty, all that was Love, all that was Truth, stood on the top of these mad mornings and sang with the stars. A great human sob shrieked in the wind, and tossed its tears upon the sea,— free, free, free.

But underneath the surface, deep down in the very soul of the new America, the hurts of war were not healed. A million men had died. The Southern whites did not like their new South. There were still big questions which had not been answered: Could the South be reconstructed? What would be the future of four and a half million ex-slaves? Would America remain a nation once unity had been achieved? But most important: Could ex-slaves and ex-masters live as equals in the same world? The answers would ultimately decide the fate of the nation.

Very few Americans in power knew what to do. Indeed America was like Hamlet, confused and undecided, not knowing whether to do what was *right* or what was *practical*. She would do neither.

Handsome Willie of Great Barrington was somewhat sheltered from these problems. Behind his New England hills he was temporarily safe. Blacks in this Berkshire town did not suffer from the obvious effects of slavery, nor would they face, as Willie was growing up, the persecution which other "colored folk" experienced. Whites in Great Barrington considered themselves democratic. Yet like most places where whites are in control, there was a color line. But the few nonwhites stayed firmly in line and never gave these democratic gentlemen reason to show their true selves. When the black people were discriminated against, it was always polite, totally consistent with the New England image of discretion. Du Bois states that there were never more than fifty blacks in a population of five thousand, and they usually kept to themselves. They entered the community in their usual menial service roles but had no influence upon the direction of the community.

The city fathers, the majority of the inhabitants, were of English and Dutch descent. They made up the upper and middle classes and were the "respectable" group which controlled the wealth and social services. The European immigrants in Great Barrington, mostly Irish and Germans, were generally powerless, uneducated, unskilled, and worked primarily as laborers in the woolen mills.

As you might expect in the North at this time in America's history, the Republican party—the party of Abraham Lincoln—was the ruling party in Great Barrington. "Indeed," as Du Bois put it, "it was not respectable to be anything else." He remarked that one of the leading lawyers was in the Democratic party, "and we suspected him of low origins and questionable designs." The men of the town took their politics rather seriously and were very involved in the open discussions which characterized the town-meeting system. The moral, ethical, and religious standards which existed were Christian and Protestant. Woman's place was in the home. Sex was never to be discussed. And typical of most American towns it was believed that through hard work, sound sleep, and prayer a good man could accomplish anything under the sun.

This is the world which shaped the young Du Bois. In a manner of speaking his roots in America were deeper than the town itself. His ancestors came to the United States in 1674. On his father's side he came from French and Haitian stock and from his mother he received his Dutch and African ancestry. Du Bois described this racial concoction rather interestingly: "a flood of Negro blood, a strain of French, a bit of Dutch, but thank God! no Anglo-Saxon." As was common in those days "most of the colored people had white blood from unions of several generations past. . . ."

It is likely that Du Bois and his family felt superior to some of the other blacks in the area. In fact Du Bois remarked, "We knew little of them but felt above them because of our education and economic status."

W. E. B. Du Bois had a typical Great Barrington boyhood. In a sense it was idyllic. Like the other lads, he ran through the woods, flew kites, climbed mountains, and explored with stick in hand hundreds of unknown caves. During the late spring and summer he fished and swam in the lakes, and in the cool New England winters he went skiing, ice skating on Lake Mansfield in the moonlight, and told stories by an open fire. Young Will Du Bois absorbed the Yankee culture very well. In fact he was quite thoroughly New England. His friends at school, because he was a brilliant student and enrolled in the college preparatory courses, were usually from the upper middle classes. Du Bois wrote, "I came in touch with rich folk, summer boarders, who made yearly excursions from New York." It was during times like these that Du Bois was confronted with racial prejudice and discrimination. His race and social origins made him different and self-conscious. Clever and witty, he defended himself well against such abuses. He struck back at the well-to-do boys by beating them at their school-work, demonstrating to them that he was their equal and most of the time their superior. But the discrimination which Du Bois felt in Great Barrington was more inconvenient than anything else and like most nineteenth-century blacks his first reaction was to ignore it. His rewards came from his outstanding scholarship and success at physical games. In fact Willie may have felt a sense of superiority over most of his white friends, since he probably felt that anyone who could discriminate on account of color had to be stupid.

In spite of these minor color episodes Du Bois shared the values of his upper-class schoolmates. Essentially he felt that hard work and ability could conquer even the worst of luck. Strongly influenced by the prevailing social thoughts during his boyhood, he believed that anyone willing to work could earn a living; those with wealth and influence deserved it, and poverty and crime were the results of laziness and immorality. His attitude about immigrants was typical: they would be all right once they became properly Americanized.

Later the man from Great Barrington would question the values he learned as a boy, but until he finished high school Du Bois was a perfect product of his environment. In fact much later he wrote ". . . had it not been for the race problem . . . I should have probably been an unquestioning worshiper at the shrine of the social order and economic development into which I was born."

In 1884, eleven years before the great abolitionist Frederick Douglass died, W. E. B. Du Bois graduated from his town's only high school. He was the only Afro-American in a class of thirteen. So it was natural that Wendell Phillips, the antislavery agitator, should have been the subject of his valedictory speech. Ambitious and somewhat of a dreamer, he had his eyes set on Harvard College. "It was the greatest and the oldest. . . . I . . . quite naturally thought it was the one I must attend. . . ." And why not? He had a good academic record and had been influenced and inspired by his white principal, Frank A. Hosmer, who had encouraged Du Bois to take those courses which would prepare him to enter college. But his dream did not come true. Harvard was too rich for his blood, and he was unable to get a scholarship.

That fall his mother died and Du Bois went to Worcester, Massachusetts, to live with his aunt. About his mother he wrote, "I felt a certain gladness to see her at peace at last, for she worried all her life. Of my own loss I had then little realization. That came only in the after years. . . . At last, I was going beyond the hills and into the world that beckoned steadily. . . . Now I was free and unencumbered and at the same time more alone than I had ever dreamed of being. . . ."

As fate would have it the opportunity to go to college came sooner than he had expected. Through the efforts of friends and church groups he was offered a scholarship to Fisk University in Nashville, Tennessee. "Disappointed though I was at not being able to go to Harvard, I merely regarded this as a temporary change of plans; I would of course go to Harvard in the end. . . ." Meanwhile Fisk would be a new experience. He would live among his own people. So in the fall of 1885, as white men in distant Germany were beginning to colonize Africa, William Edward Burghardt Du Bois went along to Fisk. It was his first trip South.

Education and Discovery

I was thrilled to be for the first time among so many people of my own color or rather of such various and such extraordinary colors, which I had only glimpsed before, but who it seemed were bound to me by new and exciting and eternal ties. Never before had I seen young men so self-assured and who gave themselves such airs, and colored men at that; and above all for the first time I saw beautiful girls. At my home among my white schoolmates there were a few pretty girls but either they were not entrancing or because I had known them all my life, I did not notice them; but at Fisk the never-to-be-forgotten marvel of that first supper came with me opposite two of the most beautiful beings God ever revealed to the eyes of 17. I promptly lost my appetite, but I was deliriously happy! Of one of these girls I have often said, no human being could possibly have been as beautiful as she seemed to my young eyes in that far-off September night. . . . Into this world I leapt with enthusiasm. A new loyalty and allegiance replaced my Americanism: henceforward I was a Negro.

Thus spoke Du Bois about his new colored world of Fisk. This university, like many other Negro colleges in the South, was founded by missionary groups shortly after the Civil War to give black people a chance at higher education. Staffed predominately by Northern white teachers, Fisk gave its eager students a heavy dose of liberal arts. No attention was paid to industrial training. The idea was to prepare the young blacks for the world by making them knowledgeable in such courses as Latin, religion, English, Greek, and etiquette.

But a good lesson on how to survive white lawless violence would probably have been more useful. The new democracy was forgotten. Lawlessness was the name of the game. Terrorist groups like the Ku Klux Klan were formed. The merciless Klan, without conscience, roamed the South whipping, tar-and-feathering, and lynching blacks. Every week, sometimes every day, there was news of lynching. Between 1885 and 1894 seventeen hundred persons of African descent were lynched. Charges were occasionally brought against the offenders, but they were even more rarely prosecuted. Everybody knew that the Klan was responsible for this violence, but no one spoke out against them.

The North closed its eyes. The South was sympathetic to the white lawbreakers. The blacks were afraid. A whole nation which called itself free closed its heart to four and a half million blacks, while the South prepared for them a new kind of servitude which would make them free in theory but slaves in practice. America was no longer confused about her direction. Her violent mouth opened, and she spoke her truth: "Prosperity to white Americans, death to the others." She proclaimed progress more important than people.

These were horrible years for the young black gentleman from Great Barrington. He had heard and read of Southern violence, but now he saw it up close. It broke into his world of innocence and nineteenth-century New England order and left his mind confused and divided. He was learning about a growing industrial civilization which was kicking his race in the face. Later he reflected, "each death was a scar upon my soul."

Fortunately all his downhome experiences were not unpleasant. Being from the North made him somewhat of a celebrity. His speech was different from his southern counterparts. He tells us in his *Autobiography* that he was stricken with a severe case of typhoid during his first weeks of school. Du Bois considered himself "a campus crisis . . . As I lay deathly sick, an orphan in a strange land, the whole school hung on the bulletin. When I crept out, thin and pale, I was the school favorite." Du Bois seemed to have identified with his fellow blacks, but many of his impressions were condescending. Undoubtedly he felt far superior to most if not all of the students. Du Bois tells us that he enjoyed his life at college. About Fisk instructors, "All of its teachers but one were white, from New England or from the New Englandized Middle West. My own culture background thus suffered no change or hiatus." But he was a campus curiosity even for the teachers and spent most of his time working on the Fisk *Herald*, the school's literary magazine, which he founded and edited. Starting his political career a bit early, he led one of the first student demonstrations in the history of Negro colleges. Du Bois and other young Turks occupied and barricaded themselves inside Jubilee Hall, the first building in the South constructed for and by black people for higher education. The outcome of the dispute is not known.

When school was out, Du Bois spent his summer vacations touring and teaching among rural, poverty-stricken blacks. These summer experiences in the hills of Tennessee had a profound effect upon his youth. He saw for the first time and became involved in the life

of the poor landless blacks. Du Bois was appalled by
the misery, poverty, and disease among these simple
folk. Not only had the new democracy failed these
people; it had also left them demoralized, frightened—
without hope. Undoubtedly these years had a permanent effect upon the direction of his life. Perhaps it
was on a lonely country road en route to a shackled
schoolhouse that Du Bois decided to devote his life to
the emancipation of his race.

In 1888, with a bachelor's degree from Fisk tucked
neatly away in his modest suitcase, Du Bois left the
land of cotton and violence and journeyed north to
Harvard. That had been his dream, now it would be
realized. But it was not what he had expected. In the
last decades of the nineteenth century this fortress of
American education was not the liberal institution it
later became. Harvard was a product of the era. Academically the school was more liberal than most colleges, but the atmosphere was rich and conservative.
Wealthy fraternity houses and exclusive eating clubs
decorated Harvard yard.

Du Bois did not see physical violence against his race
in Boston. But it was obvious to him that Harvard was
an institution of higher learning chiefly for rich Protestant gentlemen. He did not have enough money to live
in the college dormitory and because of his race he was
barred from living in the lovely buildings off campus
which housed the future rulers of America. To avoid
embarrassment, Du Bois, like the other blacks there, did

not apply to the buildings in which white students lived because he knew that he would be told, "Sorry, sir, but we have just rented our last room."

As a result of his Southern exposure, his vanishing New England idealism, and his growing knowledge of the world, the young Great Barringtonian was understandably bitter. He knew at that stage of his life what many blacks know much earlier; that he was Du Bois the Negro first, Du Bois the human being second. No doubt he would have preferred it the other way around. It would have been easier emotionally and more consistent with the so-called "spirit of individualism" of his day. But his experience had made him racially conscious, and he tended to see the world from that point of view. "I asked nothing of Harvard but the tutelage of teachers and the freedom of the laboratory and library." Until the latter part of the 1960's this seemed to be a typical attitude of Afro-Americans who studied in predominately white universities, and much more involved than what Du Bois has told us. It is a rather interesting set of attitudes. Usually black students want to associate with white students but feel they will be rejected if they try to seek out these friendships. Many Negroes have learned the hard way. Trying to be individuals first, they naturally try to be friends with whites. When they are rejected, they protect themselves from further hurt by pretending that they don't want white friends. As W. E. B. Du Bois wrote:

Had I gone from Great Barrington high school directly to

Harvard, I would have sought companionship with the white fellows and been disappointed and embittered by a discovery of social limitations to which I had not been used. But I came by way of Fisk and the South, and there I had accepted color caste and embraced eagerly the companionship of those of my own color.

He reminisces later that although this situation annoyed him intensely, he was not unhappy nor was he resentful. "Negroes were going to break down the boundaries of race; but at present we were banded together in a great crusade and happily so. Indeed, I suspect that the prospect of ultimate full human intercourse without reservations and annoying distinctions, made me all too willing to consort with my own and disdain and forget as far as was possible that outer, whiter world." He had a full social life with his "colored friends" and made the rounds of the Boston house parties and private dances. On this social circuit he met Monroe Trotter. They became good friends, and later Trotter joined Du Bois in forming the Niagara Movement.

I sought only such contact with white teachers as lay directly in the line of my work. . . . I joined certain clubs like the Philosophical Club; I was a member of the Foxcraft dining club because it was cheap. . . . I was repeatedly a guest in the home of William James; he was my friend and a guide to clear thinking. . . .

In fact Du Bois was exposed to the most prominent scholars of those times and many of them were his teachers. He read philosophy with the eminent George

Santayana and took English literature with a "fastidious Englishman," Barrett Wendell. Although Du Bois was attracted to philosophy and literature, he was more attracted to the social sciences "as the field for gathering and interpreting that body of fact which would apply to my program for the Negro."

Naturally social intercourse with whites could not be entirely forgotten, so that now and then I joined its currents and rose or fell with them. I escorted colored girls to various gatherings, and as pretty ones as I could find to the vesper exercises, and later to the classday and commencement social functions. Naturally we attracted attention and the *Crimson* noted my girl friends; on the other part came sometimes the shadow of insult, as when at one reception a white woman seemed determined to mistake me for a waiter. . . . In general, I was encased in a completely colored world, self-sufficient and provincial, and ignoring just as far as possible the white world which conditioned it. This was self-protective coloration, with perhaps an inferiority complex, but with the belief in the ability and future of black folk.

Du Bois claimed that he was not arrogant toward whites:

I was simply not obsequious, and to a white Harvard student of my day, a Negro student who did not seek recognition was trying to be more than a Negro. The same Harvard man had much the same attitude towards Jews and Irishmen. . . . I was, however, exceptional among Negroes in my ideas on voluntary segregation; they for the most part saw salvation only in integration at the earliest moment and on almost any terms in white culture; I was firm in my criticism of white folk and in my dream of a Negro self-sufficient culture even in America. . . .

This cutting off of myself from my white fellows, or being cut off, did not mean unhappiness or resentment. I was in my early manhood, usually full of high spirits and humor. I thoroughly enjoyed life. I was conscious of understanding and power and conceited enough still to imagine, as in high school, that they who did not know me were the losers, not I. On the other hand, I do not think that my white classmates found me objectionable. I was clean, not well dressed but decently clothed. Manners I regarded as more or less superfluous, and deliberately cultivated a certain brusquerie. Personal adornment I regarded as pleasant but not important. I was in Harvard, but not of it, and realized all the irony of my singing "Fair Harvard." I sang it because I like the music, and not from any pride in the Pilgrims. . . .

In June 1890 little Willie became big Willie: he received his bachelor's degree from Harvard with honors in philosophy. He had come to Harvard, gotten his degree, and had accomplished a lifelong desire. The thought that he had more formal education than most men in the country at his age, both white and black, must have made Du Bois feel ever more apart from his race and certainly somewhat arrogant. And before the ink was dry on his second university degree he had received his third, a master of arts in history.

When his friends looked around for the young Harvard MA, who had just been elected to the American Historical Society, the ambitious Du Bois had left for

Europe. He felt that ". . . I needed to go further and that as a matter of fact I had just well begun my training in knowledge of social conditions."

Du Bois in Europe. That must have been an interesting sight. He was tall, handsome, hair receding slightly, and pleasingly cocky. I can just imagine him walking proudly like a bronze prince through the streets of Venice, Florence, Paris, southern Germany, speaking to the young children; and their parents standing by asking, "Who was that dignified gentleman?"

Indeed Du Bois loved Europe. It gave him time to think, relax, study. But most of all he got away from the madness of American racism. For Du Bois, like many people of African descent, Europe was a pleasant change. He was still a Negro but not so deeply, not so intensely; European society allowed him to express himself. He saw discrimination and experienced it also. But it was never as vicious, never as total as it had been in America.

. . . . I met men and women as I had never met them before. . . . Slowly they became, not white folks, but folks. . . . I was not less fanatically a Negro, but "Negro" meant a greater, broader sense of humanity and world fellowship. I felt myself standing, not against the world, but simply against American narrowness and color prejudice, with the greater, finer world at my back. . . .

Active and alert as always, Du Bois participated freely in European cultural affairs. Since he was studying at the University of Berlin, most of his activities were centered around Germany. The young New Englander loved Germany very much. Wherever he went, he found friendship and someone to talk with. It must have blown his mind—to meet white people who "with me, did not regard America as the last word in civilization." It surely made him feel good—even though he had two—when he discovered that the University of Berlin did not recognize Harvard degrees in the same way that Harvard did not recognize Fisk degrees. "Sometimes their criticism got under even my anti-American skin, but it was refreshing on the whole to hear voiced my own attitudes toward so much that America had meant to me."

Allowed to relax and feel himself as an individual, Du Bois began thinking seriously about race relations. This was extremely difficult to do in America because he was too involved emotionally. Du Bois wanted to view the race question scientifically, being objective without being detached. In Germany his mind was clearer, his thoughts more coherent, and his actions were more creative. The University was an added encouragement. It had a great library, a progressive and dynamic intellectual community, and as he had been at Harvard, Du Bois was exposed to the leading thinkers of his day. Such men as Rudolf Virchow, Max Weber, and Adolf Wagner were his instructors. "Under these teachers and in this social setting, I began to see the race problem in America, the problem of the peoples of Africa and Asia as one." For Du Bois white racism was the same whether practiced in Europe, Asia, Africa, or

America. Also he met a few Africans and Asians and had an opportunity to share and exchange experiences with them. Until then Du Bois had taken for granted that racial harmony could be achieved politically, through education. Now he was not sure. He was searching for new directions, new answers.

Du Bois was in Europe from 1892 to 1894. He was now twenty-six and wiser and had found a society which had allowed him to partially do his thing. In a way he had lived and relived his youth and had found people who thought that the African in his skin could be beautiful. This experience shook Du Bois's world. He was exposed to socialistic ideas and values which became the intellectual foundation for his ultimate break with America.

When it is finally ours, this freedom, this liberty,
    This beautiful
and terrible thing, needful to man as air,
usable as the earth; when it belongs at last to our
    children,
when it is truly instinct, brainmatter, diastole, systole,
reflex action; when it is finally won; when it is more
than the gaudy mumbo jumbo of politicians:
this man, this Douglass, this former slave, this Negro
beaten to his knees, exiled, visioning a world
where none is lonely, none hunted, alien,
this man, superb in love and logic, this man
shall be remembered—oh, not with statues' rhetoric,
not with legends and poems and wreaths of bronze alone,
but with the lives grown out of his life, the lives
fleshing his dream of the needful beautiful thing.

ROBERT HAYDEN

The Great Black Way

The preceding poem, although written about Frederick Douglass, reflects much of Du Bois's thought at that time. Du Bois felt upon his return from Europe that America had changed very little. Lynching was at high tide. The blacks of America were still standing before the woman of justice hoping that she would take off her blindfold and look into their eyes.

Du Bois had come home singing songs and reciting verse from another land, only to be disillusioned with

America. "I felt as though the bottom of the universe was loose and I might go down." The dreams of Europe, of freedom and of individualism were over. To protect himself from white hatred he had to be a self-conscious Negro again, lose the individualism which he had acquired abroad, and become a frightened man hating America, waiting for someone to call him a nigger.

But he could not wallow in self-pity and alienation. He had his work ahead of him, and he needed all the optimism he could muster. Somehow he must have thought: We can make it; we must keep getting up. The spring of freedom will come soon.

Without money and eager to teach, Du Bois applied to several Negro colleges. "I wrote to no white institutions—I knew there were no openings." Howard, Hampton, Tuskegee, and his own Fisk turned him down. Most Negro colleges in those days wanted white teachers or Negroes with Ph.D's. Even today this is the thinking of many predominantly black institutions.

As the months passed by he received more rejections. Finally an offer came from Wilberforce, a small Methodist college and normal school in Ohio. Du Bois quickly accepted. Later that summer he got an offer to go to Booker T. Washington's Tuskegee to teach mathematics. It is likely that the history of black Americans might have been different if Du Bois had gone to Tuskegee Institute in Alabama. The Washington–Du Bois controversy (which later shaped the development of the black political struggle) might not have occurred.

So Du Bois, with German cane and gloves and idealist

expectations about what a college should be, made his way to the Midwest. The college was an intellectual desert. Nothing worked. Inefficiency ran amok. The already rigid religious restrictions were increased by compulsory religious revival meetings which often caused classes to be canceled. Du Bois's energy and scholarship added much life to the campus. But he was ahead of his time. Very few students and instructors understood his program, and his arrogance and self-importance didn't help the situation at all. As Du Bois said himself, "I was cocky and self-satisfied. . . . I doubtless strutted, and I certainly knew what I wanted. My redeeming feature was infinite capacity for work and terrible earnestness, with appalling and tactless frankness."

But the young Du Bois made the best of a bad scene. He organized the library (a few old books from the attic). He brought a bit of style to this wasteland, and once or twice Paul Laurence Dunbar, the famous black poet, came over from Dayton, Ohio, to read his poetry.

Probably Du Bois's greatest moment and perhaps his salvation was his romance with Nina Gomer—a slender, quiet dark-eyed creature who later became his wife. But love and marriage were not enough. Wilberforce was killing Du Bois spiritually, and he was suffering intellectually because he was not able to do any meaningful research in the social sciences. Two years had been almost too much.

Then it happened. In the fall of 1896 Du Bois got the break he was waiting for: an offer from the University of Pennsylvania inviting him to become an assistant instructor to work on a project involving the Philadelphia Negro. Du Bois, who had received his doctor's degree from Harvard a year earlier, did not like his title or the absence of his name from the University staff catalogue. But he saw this as a wonderful opportunity to begin his research on the study of Negro life and culture.

Dr. Du Bois dove enthusiastically into his research. For more than a year he and other researchers studied intensively the Negro ward in Philadelphia, interviewing several thousand residents. In 1899, out of this tremendous research, came Du Bois's second book, *The Philadelphia Negro*. Like his first book, *The Suppression of the African Slave Trade to the United States of America, 1638–1870*, this book was praised in some quarters, rejected in others, and ignored by some.

Scholars today, however, agree that it was his best work. Even the conservative *Yale Review* was forced to admit that *The Philadelphia Negro* rolled back the frontiers of knowledge. Anticipating what many sociologists were to say decades later, Du Bois explored and examined in great detail the problems of black people living in urban areas. He pointed out seventy years ago that problems of unemployment, self-hatred, wasteful expenditures, and malnutrition were the cause of racial backwardness. He struck an intellectual blow to those theories which had held that blacks were unable to make progress because of some biological deficiencies.

This study further elucidates Du Bois's leadership theories. He believed that the black race had to develop a Negro aristocracy which would push the race forward. He reasoned that this aristocracy, the elite of the race, could be created by formally educating ten per-cent of the race. This group would constitute the mid-dle and upper classes in black life. From this point of commitment they would develop realistic and viable alternatives to the white man's exploitation of the Negro working class. Du Bois called this group the Talented Tenth.

Consistent with his idea to create a black social sys-tem within America, he wrote that blacks should control the institutions in their communities while also getting financial aid and technical assistance from whites. Du Bois was not preaching black separation but what social scientists now call cultural pluralism. That is to say people of different ethnic backgrounds live together on a basis of equality and mutual respect, sharing and giv-ing to the greater America but retaining their sepa-rate ethnic characteristics.

The whites rejected cultural pluralism. They wanted separation, but not on the basis of equality. Du Bois argued these points before the turn of the twentieth century. They would be debated again and again for the next seventy years. They were truly problems of the twentieth century.

In 1897 the young Harvard Ph.D. returned to the South. He was invited to Atlanta University by Horace Bumstead to organize a sociology department and con-tinue his studies of Negro life and culture. Dr. Bumstead, also a New Englander, shared Du Bois's belief that only the exceptional Negroes could help the race progress.

Dr. Du Bois felt nostalgic when he saw the landscape of Atlanta. The hills reminded him of the hills of Great Barrington. Sometimes he would go for long walks and stand on a hilltop, or run until he was exhausted, and then finally breathe in deeply the fragrance of the grass until he had gotten his wind back. He could listen to the laughter of the water, write poems about the noontide, or take his wife for a quiet late evening stroll. He found peace and beauty in Atlanta, "the hurry and laughter of young hearts, winter twilight . . . one never looks for more; it is all here, restful, all intelligible."

Academically Du Bois couldn't have been happier. He did extensive scientific research into black institutions ranging from family structures to labor organizations. The young doctor was also concerned with black business, voluntary associations, and ultimately how the black man would survive in an ever-changing world.

Dr. Du Bois was exploring a new field of knowledge, and like most men who take first steps, he was constantly going against established theories and being criticized by scholars who did not take his work seriously. Like most energetic adventurers, he made mistakes, and some of his findings were confused and contradictory; but in general his undertakings were successful. A noted black sociologist, Horace Bond, has said that Du Bois's work at Atlanta "represents his efforts to introduce systematic induction into the field of race relations when other men were speculating about Negroes." Du Bois's studies went a long way to dispel some of the stereotypes held about black people. For example Du Bois disproved the assumption that whites were the main benefactors of black education by showing that blacks paid a substantial proportion of the property taxes and other indirect taxes that were used for education.

One of his most significant achievements at this time was his pioneering work in African studies. Most Americans, scholars included, viewed Africans as primitive, without culture or civilization. Indeed Africans were thought to be a group of high-level monkeys. And the best thing for them was ripe bananas and paternalistic whites, like the soon to be invented Tarzan, who in his semi-literacy would protect the natives from other corrupt white men and women.

Du Bois's work exposed these racist theories about Africa and showed that ancient Egypt was a Negro civilization. The Atlanta studies brought clarity to a very complex field and began to show the patterns of African cultural and linguistic development. Again no one but a few scholars took him seriously. The Atlanta studies have widespread appeal today, but the American public was not psychologically ready to see the image of the Negro altered.

From the beginning Du Bois was not interested in research for its own sake. Through research he preached his propaganda and his ideas that social reforms could be achieved through an understanding of social science. The Atlanta studies did little to improve the actual conditions of blacks but gave them a sense of pride and a psychological lift.

Dr. Du Bois's years at Atlanta University were very meaningful. He began to separate the real world from the world he wanted, although he never totally lost the idealism of his youth or his belief that man could and would be better. He learned a great deal about human behavior, became less detached, and dropped a lot of his New England aloofness, a trait which had to some extent set him apart from the more spirited blacks in the South.

Du Bois versus Washington

All black schoolchildren in the South hear the name Booker T. Washington at least a hundred times before they reach the ninth grade. They are told that he was a great man, a child of destiny, a leader of his people. "Cast down your bucket where you are," Booker T. Washington's celebrated saying, is one of the early things which they memorize. When they see pictures of black leaders, his face is always included. When they learn about the making of American history, Booker T. Washington's deeds are always recounted. Almost every Southern city, town, hamlet, and village has a Booker T. Washington school, park, laundry, movie, choir, band, store, or marketplace, and invariably it is called Booker T. for short. Until very recently, he,

Jesus, Buster Crabbe, and Abe Lincoln were the greatest heroes among the black working class. No other name is connected so intimately with the development of Negro life and history. Around the turn of the century Washington was probably even more famous. To understand W. E. B. Du Bois we have to know something about Booker T. Washington.

Unlike Du Bois, Booker T. was born in the South to a slave woman about four years before the Emancipation Proclamation. His father was the kind of white man who practiced nighttime integration with black women. A few years later a black man fell in love with his mother, married her, and took them to the soft-coal district of Malden, West Virginia. Since child labor was permitted in those days, Booker T. worked in the mines alongside his stepfather.

Booker was a very hard worker, and between working at home and in the mines he attended school sessions. When he finished public school, he traveled from Malden to Hampton, Virginia, to attend Hampton Institute. After graduating from Hampton, he returned to Malden to teach.

Hard work, a bit of luck, and a growing dedication to his race finally carried Booker T. to Alabama; and through constant efforts he created and established Tuskegee Institute. The Institute was primarily concerned with teaching the young black students such trades as brickmaking, carpentry, printing, tailoring, dressmaking, blacksmithing, harness-making, shoemaking, plumbing, millinery, mattress-making, and of course such things as laundering and domestic science.

Within a few years Tuskegee became one of the most famous training schools in the United States. And Booker T. Washington emerged not only as its spokesman but was considered by most whites and blacks of the day as the spokesman of the nation's ten million Afro-Americans. Indeed between 1899 and 1905 the empire builder from Tuskegee was the most sought after Negro in America. He traveled abroad and met many distinguished personalities and statesmen in Europe. During these years he received honorary degrees from Harvard and Dartmouth colleges and eventually became an adviser to Theodore Roosevelt and William Taft. What Booker T. said was important. In fact Tuskegee became the "White House" for Negro Affairs, and Mr. Washington became "head-nigger-in-charge."

What did Booker T. Washington believe? Reduced to its barest essentials his philosophy was that blacks could become first-class citizens by becoming an effective labor force. Once they had gained a degree of economic independence, they would have the power and money to apply pressure for change on the white government. For this reason Tuskegee emphasized industrial, clerical, and manual training and discouraged the teaching of the traditional liberal arts. Washington spoke for those in America who felt that politics and agitation for social reform were not the fields in which blacks should concentrate to further their cause. He was not opposed to Negro suffrage and other freedoms granted under the Constitution, but he felt that learning a useful trade would put the ex-slave in a better position to bargain collectively for these and other rights.

Some rich whites in both the North and South approved of Mr. Washington's program. For the North would have additional labor power for its growing industries, and the South would not have to worry about blacks entering politics or threatening the power and privilege of white Southern power, as they had done for a short period during the Reconstruction. Tuskegee was constantly supplied with Northern money, legal assistance, and advisers. The racist government of Alabama, which constantly ignored the Constitution, voted Booker T.'s trade school an annual appropriation.

W. E. B. Du Bois rejected the program which Washington put forward. He had different ideas about how black folk should make social, economic, and political progress. Influenced by his studies, especially those on Philadelphia and Atlanta, the young Harvard man felt that higher education in the liberal arts was the only way out of poverty and second-class citizenry. If ten percent of the race received proper higher education, this Talented Tenth would lead the black masses to the promised land. Although he agreed that the masses should be trained in trade and industrial skills in order to secure work, he believed that the ex-slave's educational program would create a docile black working class which would inevitably be led and exploited by white folk.

Also, and unlike Washington, Du Bois laid heavy

emphasis on political reform. He felt that blacks should fight uncompromisingly for the vote and if necessary return violence for violence.

In 1903 Dr. Du Bois published probably his best-known book, *The Souls of Black Folk*. In this personalized account of race relations Du Bois states his philosophy of the black man's plight in beautiful, moving prose. The book contains a harsh, critical chapter on Mr. Washington's training program which caused the rift between the two giants to deepen.

As time went on the great debate became more hostile. Each side accused the other of dishonesty, opportunism, and total disregard for the needs of future blacks. As the controversy escalated, each side became bitter and suspicious of the other. People who had previously been friends now became enemies over the Du Bois–Washington debate.

Friends on each side tried to get the two most powerful black men of the day together, but all attempts proved fruitless. They met on several occasions, had frank discussions, but could not reach a workable agreement. Neither would relinquish his position, and neither would give up any ground.

Yet as we look back to those post-Reconstruction years we find that Du Bois and Washington had much more in common than they realized. Both men respected each other although the differences in their backgrounds and training hindered them from having a meaningful friendship. The Tuskegeean depended more on the goodwill of whites, but both men fought to prevent racist legislation from being enacted. And both fought to get racist laws off the books. Both men favored black nationalism or racial self-help, but Washington's nationalist program tended to be primarily economic, while Du Bois's theories encompassed political and cultural ideas. Both men were deeply committed to the black race, although Washington limited his concern to black America and Du Bois's involvement included black Africans and black West Indians.

But the views they shared were not sufficient to establish a verbal cease-fire. Their differences were too great. Du Bois eventually felt that Washington's answers to racial advancement would have the reverse effect and would create a race of blacks totally dependent on whites. Although Du Bois agreed with Washington that blacks had to move cautiously in the South, he interpreted Washington's moves as submissive and degrading to black people.

On the other side Washington felt that the "Du Bois radicals" were immature and emotionally unstable. He also felt that they were jealous of his success and that they were protesting for the sake of adventure, profit, and entertainment. At one point Washington said that the Du Bois followers would have been very unhappy if the Negro problem had been solved.

It is difficult to say who won the debate or who was right. All the facts have still not been assessed, and more research must be done. Certain issues, however, seem clear. Both men were products of their social conditioning. Du Bois was "free born" and a Harvard scholar; Washington was "slave born" and Hampton educated. Du Bois's appeal was limited to the well-educated blacks. Washington's appeal was much broader—the black masses. There were undoubtedly jealousies, resentments, feelings of superiority and inferiority, and psychological uneasiness on both sides. Men like Du Bois and his comrades must have felt that Washington lacked certain cultural advantages, and Booker T. no doubt felt that those "New England radicals" knew German poetry but nothing about the hard lessons of survival.

One evening in Ghana Dr. Du Bois summed up the controversy: "I think that maybe the greatest difference between Booker T. and myself was that he had felt the lash, and I had not."

I doubt that God is good, well-meaning, kind,
And did He stoop to quibble could tell why
The little buried mole continues blind,
Why flesh that mirrors Him must someday die,
Make plain the reason tortured Tantalus
Is baited by the fickle fruit, declare
If merely brute caprice dooms Sisyphus
To struggle up a never-ending stair.
Inscrutable His ways are, and immune
To catechism by a mind too strewn
with petty cares to slightly understand
What awful brain compels His awful hand.
Yet do I marvel at this curious thing:
To make a poet black, and bid him sing!

COUNTEE CULLEN

The Beginning of the
Civil Rights Movement

As America moved into the early years of the twentieth century, black men and women were asking to be an equal part of their country. And the answer they received was Soon, just be patient.

Du Bois and his lonely crowd of freedom fighters were becoming increasingly more disappointed by the slow pace of progress and also because they had been unable to persuade Washington and his followers to accept a more radical strategy. The Atlanta University professor was now convinced that it would be impossible to work out a meaningful compromise with Booker T., reasoning that if black men wanted to be free, they had to become their own abolitionists.

Suddenly Du Bois was weakened. His son and firstborn died. He wrote a beautiful and bitter essay about the death of his son. Although he had loved his two-year-old child very much, W. E. B. Du Bois was somewhat relieved. His son would never feel the degradation and humiliation that a black man experiences. He would never know the evils of segregation, discrimination, and prejudice. This terrible feeling for a black American sometimes divides him because he wants a son and yet he doesn't. If a son is born and the boy dies, the father says in his heart, My son is not dead, not dead but escaped and is free. . . . His soul will not be stricken by bitterness, nor will he die a living death.

Du Bois did not have long to linger over his personal tragedy. He carried the remains of his son back to Great Barrington, and there buried the young Burghardt near his grandmother.

Du Bois returned to Atlanta and continued his work. In the summer of 1905 W. E. B. Du Bois began to take positive action. With the help of twenty-nine members of the Talented Tenth Du Bois formed a group in Fort Erie, Ontario, which became known as the Niagara Movement.

The structure of the Niagara Movement was simple. It consisted of an executive committee and twelve small committees. Naturally Dr. Du Bois was the general secretary. The mood of the conference was vigorous, and the statements which came out of the discussion sounded like the call for a new American revolution. The participants all agreed that they were tired of asking white people for their rights; the time had come to demand them from white people. Eight demands stand out from the rest: (1) Manhood voting rights; (2) a free black press; (3) freedom of speech; (4) elimination of all forms of class differences based on race or color; (5) equal employment opportunities; (6) end of white superiority; (7) the recognition of human brotherhood; (8) united and wise leadership.

As was expected Booker T. Washington attempted to destroy the Niagara Movement. He was clever and had much influence and power. He first tried to buy off some of the leadership. When that was unsuccessful, the Tuskegeean tried to undermine the Movement's activities by placing spies in the group. Newspapers friendly to Mr. Washington's views attacked the Niagara men by implying that they were dangerous and subversive.

But the Niagara members held fast. They believed in their positions and had prepared themselves for an uphill fight. Du Bois tried to strengthen his organization by forming an alliance with the Constitution League, an interracial civil-rights organization founded in 1904 by John Milholland. Washington did not approve of this alliance and did everything within his power to destroy it. But again Washington was outmaneuvered. Actually the Constitution League, like the Niagara group, was not totally anti-Washington, but from Booker T.'s point of view, you were with him all the way or you were his enemy.

Du Bois and his comrades began making plans for the second Niagara conference. For publicity and sentimental value they decided to hold the conference at Harper's Ferry, where John Brown started and ended his attempt to deal a violent blow to the inhuman slave system.

The conference accomplished little. A number of resolutions condemning the Movement's enemies were passed. President Theodore Roosevelt and his Secretary of War, William Howard Taft, were singled out. One speaker attacked the Republican party for not moving fast enough on civil-rights questions. Again Washington attempted to disrupt the conference, but again he failed.

The Atlanta race riot of 1906 erupted shortly after the second conference ended. As usual many more blacks than whites were killed. Du Bois was out of Atlanta when the riot started but quickly returned when he learned about it. On the train he composed the poem "A Litany at Atlanta," in which he accused the whites of starting the fighting and indicated that only by implementing the Niagara principles could the two races live together.

By 1909 the Niagara Movement began to decline. Its program was too far ahead of its time. Booker T. Washington was the man of the day. But the Movement's failure should not blind us to its success. This was the

first group of blacks on a national level to uncondi-
tionally demand rights for black people. They educated
many blacks and whites to a policy of racial protest
and demonstrated to the nation that all Afro-Americans
were not sold on Washington's accommodationist ten-
dencies. Du Bois and his devoted followers could be
proud of their efforts in spite of the fact that Du Bois
was not always a good leader and the group itself was
never able to reach the masses of black people.

Fortunately the fall of the Niagara Movement did
not kill Du Bois politically; in fact it became the foundation of a new organization called the National Association for the Advancement of Colored People. The
NAACP was first called the Negro National Committee,
but when the Niagara veterans joined, the name was
changed. From its beginning in 1909 the group was
interracial. Most of the whites were influential Northern
liberals including such people as Oswald Garrison Vil-
lard, Lillian Wald, Jane Addams, and John Milholland.
And the blacks in the positions of leadership had been
formerly with Du Bois in the Niagara Movement.

Like the Niagara group, the new NAACP felt that
Washington's efforts at Tuskegee were insufficient.
Lynchings had increased. The Ku Klux Klan freely
roamed the South, and the federal government was
making excuses about its inaction in enforcing the Thir-
teenth, Fourteenth, and Fifteenth Amendments.

What to do about Booker T. Washington was one
of the NAACP's first questions. They did not want an
open fight with him. Washington was opposed in prin-

ciple to the formation of the new group.

Washington felt that the NAACP would encroach upon his turf. Unlike Du Bois, Washington had a following among the masses, and he no doubt felt that the new organization might threaten his power. Also, and very important, whites in the South who supported Washington's program but feared the new interracial body of northern radicals pressured Washington to destroy the new group. The NAACP tried to convince him that they could work in harmony with him, but an effective union was never established.

During the first year of its existence the NAACP faced problems both inside and outside the organization. Inside, there were administrative problems and some personality clashes. Men like Monroe Trotter felt that the new group was too white and would ultimately be controlled by whites. Outside, the young organization faced threats of violence from whites who opposed it and of course had to endure constant harrassment from the Tuskegee crowd and the newspapers which they controlled. Before these problems could be solved, World War I started and brought a new set of problems. There was an increase in lynching. Black soldiers were often rejected when they volunteered to fight for their country; and when they were accepted, they were placed in segregated fighting units. Or frequently they became servants, shoeshine boys, or cooks and stewards for the white soldiers.

The NAACP moved resolutely but slowly during these growing years. At first it showed itself to be a progressive and worthwhile group. It faced a hostile country, especially in the South, and its members' lives were always in danger. They were young, courageous, and idealistic. They walked across states preaching their message of social justice and trying to expand their membership. They wanted for black Americans all the rights which white Americans had without conditions or reservations. The group was always active, alert, and committed. Du Bois, for example, was sent to Europe during the war to investigate the treatment given to black soldiers.

But essentially the NAACP remained a middle-class organization. It concentrated on legal action, never developed a broad program for economic and social change, and therefore never really understood the actual conditions of black people. Nor was it ever able to attract the masses to its banners. In fact when the working-class black poked fun at the NAACP, he called it the Negro Assembly for the Advancement of *Certain* Colored People.

With the death of Booker T. Washington in 1915 W. E. B. Du Bois became the front runner in the cause of black liberation. For a while Tuskegee remained the vital force it had been, but without Washington's leadership it slowly fell into the background. For the first time in many years it now seemed possible that Du Bois would unite under the NAACP's banner all the groups striving for Afro-American advances.

Perceptive and alert to the political signs of the time, Dr. Du Bois quickly rallied his efforts to take advantage of this opportunity. After leaving Atlanta University, Du Bois devoted himself full time to the NAACP. He could have become its leading executive officer but instead preferred his position as editor-in-chief of *The Crisis*, the NAACP's official magazine.

The Crisis was a separate branch in the NAACP establishment; it maintained considerable independence from the board of directors and came to be known as Du Bois's private domain. Du Bois believed that a publication was an indispensable part of NAACP work, and under his influence it became an effective voice in Afro-American affairs.

The magazine was produced for a small educated Negro public. Nevertheless Du Bois tried to build up his readership by publishing articles which might appeal to a less educated audience. During the first year of *The Crisis* there were columns devoted to such things as colored high schools, women's affairs, colored sports, Harriet Beecher Stowe's "Personal Knowledge of the Negro Character," and a special feature called "Along the Color Line," which like a small-town newspaper contained the local gossip about black social life. Like most new journals, *The Crisis* carried its share of advertisements. In addition Negro college activities were announced, and there was also an important section on legal affairs.

A large proportion of the readership was mulattoes. They played an active part in the social and intellectual life of the middle-class Negro, and without undue exaggeration one could easily say that *The Crisis* was their second Bible. Many critics of Du Bois maintained that *The Crisis* appealed almost exclusively to mulattoes, pointing out that usually light-skinned Negroes were featured on the covers.

Yet if *The Crisis* was as the critics said, "a social calendar for the bright, light, and damn near white," it was also an unending militant voice protesting white status quo. Du Bois thought of himself as an adviser to his race. In his articles he attempted to explain his ideas of social justice and equality. *The Crisis* editor constantly told his readers that whites acted as they did because they feared that their race might not be superior. Professor Elliot M. Rudwick, one of Du Bois's biographers, tells us—in his well-praised study *W. E. B. Du Bois, Propagandist of the Negro Protest*—that Du Bois's writing in the magazine was frequently aphoristic, which made it easier for the readers to remember. The following sentences are examples of such writing:

"Oppression costs the oppressor too much if they stand up and protest."

"Agitate then, brother; protest, reveal the truth and refuse to be silenced."

"A moment's let up, a moment's acquiescence, means a chance for the wolves of prejudice to get at our necks."

A common target for *The Crisis* was the church, both black and white. Du Bois attacked the church for not taking a greater stand against social inequalities and in fact accused it of being the "greatest seat of racial and color prejudice." His articles accused the Negro churches of preaching fatalism and doom and suggested that they become increasingly more liberal in method and spirit.

Du Bois's editorials were lucid, straightforward, and always dramatic. He wrote, "I am resolved to be quiet and law-abiding, but to refuse to cringe in body or in soul, to resent deliberate insult, and to assert my just right in the face of wanton aggression."

On another occasion, enraged by lawless violence, *The Crisis* editor wrote, "Let black men especially kill lecherous white invaders of their homes and then take their lynching gladly like men. It's worth it."

The Crisis struck out time and time again at the horror of lynching:

Let the eagle scream! America is redeemed at Coatesville. Some people talk of punishing the heroic mob, and the governor of Pennsylvania seems to be real provoked. We hasten to assure our readers that nothing will be done. There may be a formal arrest, but the men will be promptly released by the mob sitting as jury—perhaps even as judge. America knows her true heroes.

This we said some nine months ago when the crucifixion at Coatesville was new in its horror. Some of our readers took us roundly to task at the time, but today we can proudly announce the fulfillment of our prophecy: The last lyncher is acquitted and the best traditions of Anglo-Saxon civilization are safe. Let the eagle scream!

Under the direction of the NAACP ten thousand

Afro-Americans marched down New York's Fifth Avenue on July 28, 1917, in protest against lynching. As always Du Bois used his mighty pen to draw out his enemies. After the brutal burning of several black soldiers, some of whom were even burned alive in uniform, Du Bois wrote a fiery editorial in the next issue of *The Crisis:*

"We return fighting—make way for democracy.
We saved it in France and by Great Jehovah,
We will save it in the USA, or know the reason
why. . . ."

As Du Bois's prestige increased so did his writing. By 1915 he had published seven books and thirty-eight articles. Among his books was a controversial biography, *John Brown.* In 1911 he had published a novel called *The Quest of the Silver Fleece.* In 1915 *The Negro* appeared, a study similar in quality to his earlier book *The Philadelphia Negro.*

Meanwhile on the international scene Du Bois intensified his campaign against European colonialism. A few months after the end of World War I, Du Bois, then forty-nine, sailed to Paris to become an observer at the peace talks. Although Du Bois was interested in peace, he actually went to Paris to call a meeting of the world's black leaders, a meeting which he called the Pan-African Congress. This was not the first such conference. The first had been organized in July, 1900, by a West Indian lawyer named H. Sylvester Williams.

Distinguished black men from the United States, Africa, the Caribbean, and Europe had been invited to attend, and Du Bois had been chosen to chair the Committee on the Address to the Nations of the World.

Out of this first congress came declarations denouncing colonialism and imperialism, and the delegates demanded that the European powers grant their colonies self-government "as soon as practicable." Moreover Du Bois introduced the idea that these governing powers should establish a free black state in the Congo region of Africa. Indeed after that first congress, Du Bois was one of a very few men in America who kept alive an interest in Africa. Even before the turn of the century he had protested to the Belgian Consul-General in America for her treatment of Africans in the Belgian Congo. With Belgium and other European countries Du Bois wanted to set up development programs for Africans directed by blacks from all over the world. The men of Niagara established a Pan-African Bureau and frequently corresponded with African intellectuals.

In much the same spirit the aging Harvard scholar organized the Pan-African Congress of 1919. In the beginning the NAACP did not share Dr. Du Bois's enthusiasm for the congress. Finally he persuaded its board of directors to make an official statement in support of his African view. Reluctantly the board approved.

The procedure of the second congress was of the same general nature which had characterized the first. It condemned colonial exploitation of "colored peoples" and called for peace and mutual respect among men regardless of race and creed. The League of Nations—a now defunct body similar to the United Nations that was created shortly after World War I—was warned that the African colonies which Germany had lost as a result of the war should not be handed over to another colonial power. The congress also demanded of the League that a permanent body be organized on an international level to oversee and protect the rights of Africans, especially as they related to questions of land alienation and wage exploitation. In short they wanted the League of Nations, meeting in Paris, to apply the same new standards of justice, equality, and law to Africans. Moreover the congress wanted President Woodrow Wilson's famous Fourteen Points for freedom to apply to every living person. The congress declared, "wherever persons of African descent are civilized and able to meet the tests of surrounding culture, they should be accorded the same rights as their fellow citizens."

The Paris congress gave Du Bois many headaches. Problems of organization were immense. The United States State Department refused to issue passports to certain blacks who wanted to attend. In fact some of those blacks who were unable to obtain permission to travel accused Du Bois of being a "good nigger" who had "the stamp of approval of President Wilson and his bourbon-drinking Southern democrats."

Looking back on those years, one could say that that congress accomplished little of real importance. This assessment would be partially correct. The Americans and Europeans of the 1920's, in spite of statements to the contrary, were not prepared morally, politically, or economically to yield to the demands of men like Du Bois and his idealistic band of black abolitionists. A few newspapers and many progressive whites, both in Europe and America, thought that there was "nothing unreasonable about these Ethiopian dreams." But another war and much more history would have to happen before a free and independent Africa could be realized.

Du Bois versus Garvey

Then came Marcus Garvey. Suddenly without warning this man challenged Du Bois's leadership, declaring that only *he* was the chosen prophet of the Negro cause. Coming from the West Indies, Garvey's political style was unlike that of Washington or Du Bois. Garvey had some of the best qualities of both men: Du Bois's radical vision and Washington's common touch, a fact which may account for his extraordinary popularity among the black masses.

Marcus Garvey called his movement the Universal Negro Improvement Association (UNIA), whose headquarters was in Harlem with branches in many American cities and some foreign countries. Proclaiming himself "President-in-exile of Africa," Garvey's dream was to liberate Africa from all forms of European oppression and to make it free for all Africans and all people of African descent. Believing that it was impossible for black people to receive social justice in white societies, the Jamaican advocated a "back to Africa" program for New World Africans. To accomplish his objective Garvey set up the Black Star Shipping Line and the Negro Factories Corporation.

I agree with those historians who maintain that the conflict between Garvey and Du Bois was inevitable. In spite of Du Bois's own radicalism the NAACP could not speak to the ever-growing needs of the black masses. The NAACP had achieved some impressive court victories, but the majority of blacks were not concerned with voting in white primaries, as important as that might have been. They had immediate material needs, and victories in high courts were too far removed to be of any practical benefit.

Marcus Garvey addressed himself to their needs. He promised his people a way out of poverty, discrimination, and second-class citizenship. He did not make grand speeches about freedom and abstract concepts of justice. He spoke to the black people all over the country in a language which they could understand. The Jamaican was frank and inflammatory. Garvey told his eager audiences that he would deliver them, and they waited for their savior to lead them to the Promised Land.

Partially because he did not understand Garvey's appeal and partially because he did not take him seriously, Du Bois ignored the fiery UNIA organizer. But not for long. Garvey mounted his campaign against the Talented Tenth. He accused Du Bois and his associates of deliberately ignoring the masses and worshiping the white man's symbols of progress. He said that Du Bois was constantly confused and misguided because he had white ancestors. As Garvey said so many times about Du Bois, "Sometimes . . . he is French . . . another time he's Dutch, and when it is convenient, he is a Negro." Then Garvey would go on to say about himself that he was not of mixed blood. "The men who built the pyramids looked like me, and I think the best thing I can do is to keep looking like them."

In spite of these attacks Du Bois did not retaliate in kind. Such behavior would not have been consistent with the image of refinement that Du Bois had of himself. Indeed he did not wish to fight Garvey openly. Much later Du Bois did acknowledge that Garvey had been an "honest man, sincere, hard working, dynamic, and with an unselfish desire to serve." Seeing Garvey's success with his mass movement, the editor of *The Crisis* hoped that the Jamaican might cooperate with him in realizing some of the goals for which *The Crisis* had been crusading.

But Garvey did not want a *rapprochement*. He did not trust Du Bois, and through the *Negro World*, the UNIA's publication, Garveyites continued their campaign to discredit W. E. B. Du Bois.

Garvey then took his fight to the international arena. In 1921, two weeks before Du Bois was to convene the Third Pan-African Congress, Garvey tried to steal the show by calling his own international conference in New York. There the Garveyites condemned the Du Bois Congress and called for the repudiation of his movement. The UNIA also ridiculed the Pan-African Congress because white men had been invited.

But Du Bois was unmoved. His efforts came off as planned. Meetings were held in London on August 28 and 29, in Brussels on August 31 through September 2, and in Paris on September 5 and 6. There were 113 official delegates, including 25 from America and 41 from Africa.

After the Third Pan-African Congress, Marcus Garvey continued his criticism of Du Bois. He made a point of the fact that the congress was not a "native" movement because it did not have grass-roots support and that the Du Bois movement was led by a "light-skinned, mixed blood caste aristocracy." He maintained that the UNIA was the only organization able to protect the darker skinned masses and that Du Bois's Talented Tenth would lead blacks to destruction.

Du Bois felt that Garvey placed too much emphasis on color variations within the race and that if continued this would eventually cause a schism. Yet Du Bois's characterization of Garvey was to some extent proof of Garvey's color charges. He referred to Garvey as "a little fat, black man; ugly, but with intelligent eyes and a big head." Garvey replied that he was proud of his dark color.

Finally white America resolved the Du Bois–Garvey dispute. Marcus Garvey was indicted for fraud. The government alleged that he had used the mails to sell worthless stock. Garvey's defense stated that his associates in the Black Star Shipping Line had stolen the money he had collected to purchase a ship to take black Americans back to Africa. He was convicted and later deported.

The UNIA collapsed without Garvey's leadership. By 1923 the Black Star Shipping Line and the UNIA's other business enterprises were bankrupt. The black masses were left without a steamship, without a savior —they were stuck with promises which they could never realize.

The struggle between Du Bois and Garvey left a lasting impression on the civil-rights movement. Many blacks blamed the NAACP elite for Garvey's deportation; and it was permanently branded as an exclusive group of middle-class Negroes supported by liberal northern whites.

Eventually Du Bois agreed with those who had earlier attacked the NAACP. He had seen the body moving in that direction but had been unable to move it to the left of center. He also changed his views about Marcus Garvey. He came to see Garvey as an important figure in the history of the civil-rights struggle, especially his ability to recruit the masses of black people. It was ironic that Du Bois should go where Garvey wanted to take all black people. And not just to any place in Africa, but to Ghana and to Kwame Nkrumah, who claimed that Garvey had influenced him more than any other man.

If we must die—let it not be like hogs
Hunted and penned in an inglorious spot,
While round us bark the mad and hungry dogs,
Making their mock at our accursed lot.
If we must die—Oh, let us nobly die,
So that our precious blood may not be shed
In vain; then even the monsters we defy
Shall be constrained to honor us though dead!
Oh, Kinsmen! We must meet the common foe;
Though far outnumbered, let us show us brave,
And for their thousand blows deal one deathblow!
What though before us lies the open grave?
Like men we'll face the murderous, cowardly pack,
Pressed to the wall, dying, but fighting back!

CLAUDE MCKAY

The Crash

The preceding poem by Claude McKay expresses the mood, the postwar restlessness, of black America. McKay was not the only person to capture the tempo of the era. The years following World War I were very productive for black intellectuals. There was an unprecedented outpouring of literature, art, and music. So expressive was this period that it is referred to as the "Negro Renaissance."

"Disdaining economic considerations and unconcerned

about the approval of whites," the black artists of the twenties were concerned above all with expressing their own feelings in their own way. In poetry the best known were Langston Hughes, Claude McKay, and Countee Cullen. In the field of the novel, writers such as Jessie Fauset, Jean Toomer, and Rudolph Fisher were discovered in the twenties. And in music jazz emerged as a distinct art form. Other personalities involved in these movements were such people as E. Franklin Frazier, a noted Howard University sociologist; J. A. Rogers, a historian; Alain Locke, a gifted writer and historian; Paul Robeson, an actor-writer-singer; Roland Hayes, singer-dancer; Bill Robinson; and Duke Ellington.

W. E. B. Du Bois was an important ingredient in the development of this artistic movement. Using his critical and analytical skills, he attempted to create a unifying cultural philosophy which would give the artistic renaissance an overall self-definition. According to historian Harold Cruse in his *Crisis of the Negro Intellectual*, "Dr. Du Bois went on to describe Negro art in its functional relationship to the civil-rights movement, and its aim as a Negro cultural expression within the context of the American nationality idea." Moreover the rise of this new artistic movement owed much to the pioneering sociological work which Du Bois had started years earlier.

That race pride which underpinned the creative expression of those black writers and musicians resulted in part from their awareness of the historical role Afro-Americans had played in America. In the twenties, as never before, blacks began to look back to the past and were starting to realize that their roots cut deep in America and that they had made a significant contribution to its history and culture.

The Crisis became synonymous with the black renaissance. It was like a literary bulletin board introducing, interpreting, and explaining the new black art to those looking to understand it. *The Crisis* introduced the painters Richard Brown and Wilbur Scott and discovered Jessie Fauset and Langston Hughes. Du Bois announced the formation of a phonograph-record company dedicated to supporting Afro-American musical artists and proposed to establish "an Institute of Negro Literature and Art for the purpose of association, recognition, and mutual criticism." As Elliot Rudwick maintained, "No Negro writer could help but have been stimulated by *The Crisis* editor's lyrical and plaintive pieces." Du Bois said himself in *The Crisis*, "Practically every Negro author writing today found his first audience through the pages of *The Crisis*."

But the new artistic movement did not live. The development of the mass communications media and the black creative artists' acceptance of the concept of an integrated theater caused the destruction of a creative Harlem, the intellectual and artistic capital of the black world. Harold Cruse tells us that there was nothing wrong with striving for integration on moral and ethnical grounds, but integration became an end in itself. Those blacks who desired it rejected Du Bois's concept of cultural pluralism and did not press for political, economic, and cultural autonomy. This destroyed the only base upon which an authentic Afro-American art form could survive.

In short the Negro renaissance never took root in America because middle-class Negroes did not support it. Like their white counterparts, they loved the excitement of the performers but never took their work seriously as art. And since they did not support the creative movement, they did not control it. This meant that the control and direction of this tremendous talent of dancers, comedians, composers, writers, choreographers, and singers fell into the hands of white promoters and theater-owners. These men exploited black talent, profiting by the millions while at the same time eliminating Harlem as a cultural center. About Harlem today and about other black communities Cruse reminds us, "The Harlem Community as a whole must adapt for itself the concept of cooperative and collective economic organization and administration of its inner community life, or else the Negro's chances for survival in the U.S. are very slim."

Meanwhile Dr. Du Bois continued his struggle for first-class citizenship. *Darkwater*, which Du Bois called his "semi-biography," stirred up considerable controversy when it was published in 1920. Segments of the white literary establishment considered it inflammatory and accused Du Bois of preaching violence and racial hatred. One leading magazine, *Nineteenth Century and After*, interpreted the book to mean that the black world was preparing for war against the white world.

Naturally Du Bois was misunderstood. True he was angry for the millionth time about the treatment of his race, but on the whole his indictment of the white race was rather mild. He set the tone of the book in the first few pages under a section called "Credo":

I believe in God, who made of one blood all nations that on earth do dwell. I believe that all men, black and brown and white, are brothers, varying through time and opportunity, in form and gift and feature, but differing in no essential particular, and alike in soul and the possibility of infinite development.

Does that sound violent or inflammatory? In fact if you add the word *dream* in a few places, it would sound like a speech the late Martin Luther King might have given.

Beyond *Darkwater*, *The Crisis* editor intensified his attack upon the establishment, both black and white. He accused the Negro colleges like Fisk, Hampton, Lincoln, and Howard (which he hoped would be a showplace and demonstrate to the world that blacks could successfully operate a great institution) of not taking any real interest in the race issues. Fisk and several other colleges were singled out either for being too concerned with white Southern sentiment or for not having more Negroes on the faculty and in administrative positions.

On the economic front he called for a serious reorganization of black business. "Properly managed and advised, the Talented Tenth could eliminate poverty in the urban areas by financing large-scale building projects," Du Bois said. He felt that the businesses should not be established on traditional capitalistic lines and advised blacks with capital to establish "consumer cooperation" stores. Two principles were intended to set the stores apart from the usual businesses. First, people would receive profits in proportion to how much they purchased, not in relationship to how much stock they held. Second, all members would have one vote regardless of how much stock they owned. Du Bois was not unaware of the hazards of such ventures. He knew, for example, that the black middle class, like its white counterpart, was profit-oriented and would exploit the black masses if they had a chance. But being optimistic and idealistic he felt that the mass of black people would in the long run profit from these racial enterprises.

Influenced by his notions of Pan-Africanism, Dr. Du Bois proposed a black cooperative economic system which would include Afro-Americans, West Indians, Africans, and people of African descent living in Europe. But he found little support for his black-power advocacy. Once again the rising black middle class of the early 1920's did not see the need for such ventures. They were not seeking a separatist solution to their problems at this level. They wanted integration into the established white economy and their rightful place in the promised land of the American mainstream. One can only say that they were taken in by the democratic rhetoric of the twenties and by America's ultimate power to redeem and save their lives.

In 1926 Du Bois shocked many who didn't understand him and pleased his enemies when he visited the Soviet Union. Professor Rudwick tells us that Du Bois made a sharp turn to the left, implying that by then Du Bois was taking orders from the Kremlin.

Rudwick's observations are misleading. Dr. Du Bois was offered a trip to visit Russia. He accepted but made it clear that the visit would not in any way commit him to Soviet propaganda. He did not want to be misunderstood because he did not want international involvement to jeopardize his domestic programs and appeals.

But he desperately wanted, as the Ghanaians say, "to go see." Since his student days in Germany, W. E. B. Du Bois had been fascinated by the writings of Karl Marx and Frederick Engels. Later he had considered himself a socialist and had followed some of his white friends, Mary Ovington, Charles Edward Russell, and William English Walling, into the American Socialist party.

Perhaps he was sympathetic to some of the Soviet Union's plans for modernization, but at the same time he seemed to express strong objections to others. Looking back to those post-World War I years, three reasons for the visit seem to stand out. First, as a student of societies he wanted to see what, if anything, the revolution had accomplished. And being a propagandist himself, he knew that he was not getting an objective assessment from Western sources, which were explicitly hostile to the Bolshevik government in Russia. Second, he assumed that his trip would make the State Department a little uneasy, a balance to strengthen his bargaining position with the United States government when he returned. And last, like any sensible person, he took advantage of a paid vacation. Given his heavy schedule, he surely needed the rest.

Later W. E. B. Du Bois wrote about the historic visit:

My visit to Germany and the Soviet Union in 1926 and then to Turkey and Italy on returning brought a change in my thoughts and actions. . . . I saw, of course, but little in one short month. I came to no conclusions as to whether that particular form of the Russian state was permanent or a passing phase. . . . What amazed and uplifted me in 1926 was to see a nation stoutly facing a problem which most other modern nations did not dare even to admit was real: the abolition of poverty.

To balance his general praise of Soviet achievements Du Bois assured his *Crisis* readers that all was not perfect behind the curtain of iron. Du Bois did not in 1926 advocate the Russian brand of communism as a program of change for the United States. He did not believe that the Communist party's program could solve the problems of black America.

Without a doubt he supported the development of socialism along peaceful lines. He believed that "production should be for *use* and not for *profit* and that there should be a greater sharing of the wealth."

Up until he officially joined the Communist party in 1961 Du Bois appears to have supported the Marxist theory of history but probably did not accept in totality

Marx's notion that the workers would be the vanguard of the revolution. Intellectually Du Bois was interested in Marx's philosophy because it was one of protest and because it promised the full realization of man's humanity. Practically Du Bois was also interested in short-term gains for his people. And to that extent he clung to his ideas of cultural pluralism and the Talented Tenth.

Often he advocated black business as a solution for the masses of black people, but he also maintained with equal force that Afro-Americans should "work in conjunction with the most intelligent body of American thought, and that in the future as in the past, out of the mass of American Negroes would arise a far-seeing leadership in lives of economic reform."

In the presidential election of 1928 Du Bois supported the Socialist candidate, Norman Thomas, but attacked the Socialist party in the South because it barred blacks from membership in deference to white recruits.

Du Bois admitted that capitalism had created the racial problems but rejected doctrinaire Marxism as an answer to the problem. He also accused the Communists of using the blacks for their own purposes. In 1931 Du Bois, supported by the NAACP, said that the Communists wanted the Scottsboro boys (nine blacks accused of raping two white girls) to be executed in order to use their death for propaganda. Many Afro-Americans joined Du Bois in his early rejections of communism and socialism.

In Du Bois's final writings he does not accept the notion that his views were then inconsistent.

"It was clear to me that agitation against race prejudice and a planned economy for the bettering of the economic condition of the American Negro were not antagonistic ideals, but part of one ideal. . . ." He further contends that he was not preaching separatism: "Segregation was there and would remain for many years. . . ." His plan "would not establish a new segregation; it did not advocate segregation as the final solution of the race problem, exactly the contrary." What he claimed in effect was that self-help programs for blacks were not advocating separation but a necessary step in the move to social justice, apparently in a fully integrated socialistic society.

Perhaps. Maybe the more important question to consider (which might shine more light on Du Bois's own attitudes) is why did most Afro-Americans, who made no clear distinctions between socialism and/or communism, reject the left-wingers who shouted to them: "Come join us"? Were they not the ones who would have benefited most under the so-called new freedom? Why did they remain loyal to a system which had made them slaves and later second-class human beings? Moreover Professor Benjamin Quarles in *The Negro in the Making of America* tells us that leftist whites actually practiced what they preached:

Another tactic to win Negroes was that of practicing social equality. Communists ate with Negroes, went on outings with them, and lived in the same apartment buildings, all in an effort to make the Negro feel a complete personal acceptance. Still another part of their program was designed to push Negroes to the fore by giving them responsible positions in the Party and running them for high offices on the Party ticket in state and national elections.

Beyond that the Communists provided black artists with creative outlets, organized the American Negro Labor Congress in 1925 (which was designed to strengthen black labor), and in the same year organized the International Labor Defense, "concerned primarily with cases involving Afro-Americans, irrespective of their party affiliations." And two black men, A. Philip Randolph and Chandler Owen, jointly edited a Socialist publication called the *Messenger*.

Yet the leftist movement had few black converts. Again we must turn to Quarles:

The Socialist Party made little impression upon the Negroes. Although the entire Socialist program revolved around the workingman, the Party was unable to make a special appeal to the Negro. Viewing the problems of society as primarily economic rather than racial, they saw the Negro primarily as a worker and only incidentally as black. No matter how eloquent, their program was viewed by the Negro as a bit remote from his immediate needs.

In essence the blacks did not feel a sense of gratitude to the followers of Karl Marx. A presidential poll published in 1932 by *Opportunity* magazine showed that 51 blacks out of 3,973 polled planned to support the Communist party nominee. Blacks did not seem to buy the Communist message. They were radical on issues which were *directly* related to race, but otherwise, as Quarles says, "the Negro was a man of conservative mold." The Communists had said many new and interesting things, but they also criticized many ideas, especially religious, which many Afro-Americans believed. Like most Americans, blacks were individualistic and the Communist dogma turned them off. Again like most whites, they were practical, middle class in outlook, and skeptical about all utopias except heaven. They would take their chances with the devil they knew.

Coming of Age

The dead and outworn husk of the America that had been cracked and split right down the back, and the living, changing, suffering thing within—the real America, the America that had always been, the America that was yet to be—began slowly to emerge . . . the leaders of the nation had fixed their gaze so long upon the illusion of a false prosperity that they had forgotten what America looked like.

Thusly did Thomas Wolfe describe the Depression. An economic empire had collapsed: the crash was heard throughout the world. It was loud, ugly, destructive, and complete. No class, creed, race, or religion was spared. The fall of Wall Street in 1929 brought fear to the face of America.

Black Americans looked on. The crash was white man's business, but they would share in the misery of

the Depression. Made conscious by their own imprisonment, they had always seen the face that Wolfe was
now finding the courage to describe. Wolfe called it
alienation. To them is was just plain evil. As always they
would suffer more than whites. They knew that. They
were the last to be hired, the first to be fired. They were
ready for anything. They would endure. Because they
knew, deep down in their souls, what maybe no other
white man knew, what Wolfe knew, that "through it all,
there was only one certainty. . . . America was still
America, and whatever new thing came of it, it would be
America."

Du Bois tells us:

The story of the Depression as it affected American Negroes, has not yet been adequately attempted. In many
great centers of population more than a third of the Negroes
went on public charity and more ought to have gone,
but suffered deliberate discrimination in the South. . . . The
greater tragedy was the loss of thousands of farms and
homes, the disappearance of savings among the rising Negro
middle class [and] the collapse of Negro businesses—banks,
insurance companies, and retail businesses.

As fear and panic increased, the black man became
the logical scapegoat. Whites replaced blacks in certain
industrial jobs. As Du Bois recounts, "in the matter of
reemployment and readjustment after the Depression, the
first duty of white Americans was toward white folk."
And for those blacks who found it difficult to adjust to
the emergency condition, the Ku Klux Klan (which

flourished once again, both in the North and in the South) gave special courses in whipping, lynching, and subservience.

During this time Du Bois was engaged in a desperate power struggle with the executive board over the control and direction of *The Crisis*. The struggle was inevitable. Du Bois had moved the magazine further to the political left, and it clashed with the board's increasing conservatism. Under normal conditions the struggle would have dragged on at an irritating but not disrupting level, but the Depression brought the opposing sides into open warfare.

Like most businesses which survived the aftermath of the Depression, the NAACP was in a tight financial strain. Many new programs had been abandoned, and existing programs had to be streamlined. *The Crisis* was in the latter group. For twenty-three years under the editorship of Du Bois it had been, as the editor said, "an independent organ leading a liberal organization toward radical reform."

Symbolically, if not actually, *The Crisis* was a child of Du Bois. His sweat and energy created it; his ideas and talents sustained it; and before the rise of the urban Negro press his vision had made *The Crisis* the secular gospel for the black reading public. Although Du Bois was paid by and answerable to the executive board, he had broad power; he had been allowed to operate the journal without interference and had virtual control over all its funds. In short he did exactly what he wanted to do.

But times were changing. The whites and blacks who called the shots in the NAACP wanted to take the body in a new direction, a practical direction, without criticism from the body's left-wing members. The executive board wanted to adopt Du Bois's *Crisis* and assume all responsibilities for its future growth. Naturally Du Bois said no. Like any father he was concerned about the health and welfare of his child. He had nurtured it on one set of ideas and saw no reason to change the formula; and he felt that a good dose of conservatism might strangle the organ. According to him the board "represented largely capital and investment and only to a small degree labor and socialism."

But the position which the board took was prompted solely by political considerations. Du Bois a fine editor, but in truth the gentleman from Barringt was a poor administrator. The magazine had been steadily losing money, and the already high production costs had increased. And with the appearance of other black news media *The Crisis* was in serious trouble. So the board reasoned that under new management *The Crisis* might solve both its financial and political problems.

To make matters worse Du Bois found it extremely difficult to communicate with Walter White, the new executive secretary who succeeded James Weldon Johnson. Du Bois described Mr. White as a very fair-skinned Negro who represented the thinking of the conservative board, as "absolutely self-centered and egotistical to the point that he was almost unconscious of it." One scholar said that the conflict between the two men was bound to happen because Dr. Du Bois had finally found a man lighter in skin complexion and more arrogant than he.

As the verbal battle raged Walter White's position became stronger. Finally Du Bois was outmaneuvered. At the end of 1932 Du Bois's life's work was reorganized into the Crisis Publishing Company, and Walter White was made director of the new company.

Du Bois bitterly fought this restructuring, but he did not hold the right tool. Unable to continue his own way Du Bois took a leave of absence and accepted a professorship at his old college, Atlanta University. After a stormy year of fighting, Du Bois resigned in 1934 from the civil-rights organization which he had helped form.

With Du Bois out of the way many black intellectuals both inside and outside of the NAACP analyzed but rejected Du Bois's theories of cultural pluralism and community control. These younger men felt that building a Negro economy was impractical since blacks were without the manufacturing and distributing skills needed to succeed in big business. Ralph Bunche felt that the self-help notion was insane because "the legal and police force of the State would inevitably . . . be against them." According to Rudwick, "James Weldon Johnson considered that the Negro's success would only make whites envious and therefore even more suppressive in their treatment of the blacks."

Hence the policy of the NAACP became oriented toward the Negro business-professional classes, who, according to Rudwick, "wanted the NAACP to retain its traditional emphasis on political–civil equality, because

in these areas they were the main victims of racial discrimination." The black masses were not seriously considered since the Negro businessmen had refused to adopt
the trade-union orientation intended to advance the
economic interest of these forgotten masses. Incredible
as it may seem the ideas and policies of the present-day
NAACP are the result of these early 1930 decisions.
And the battle between those policies and cultural pluralism continues.

I, too, sing America.

I am the darker brother.
They send me to eat in the kitchen
When company comes,
But I laugh,
And eat well,
And grow strong.

Tomorrow,
I'll be at the table
When company comes.
Nobody'll dare
Say to me,
"Eat in the kitchen,"
Then.

Besides,
They'll see how beautiful I am
And be ashamed—

I, too, am America.

LANGSTON HUGHES

A Second Life

Some men are dead by sixty-six. Some are too old to live; they are crippled, walking slow, bent over in pain, or waiting with their medication in some dismal rest home, waiting patiently, for the next stage of life. At sixty-six the ex-*Crisis* editor was still in great shape: functional, alert, shoulders straight. And his eager mind was in search of more projects and more action. He was very much alive.

Each year of his life cried out, cried out for more life

—a cry of birth resounding in his dark soul, keeping him young and fit, never allowing him to think old. Of the vibrant Du Bois one might have said:

His soul was ready
But he could not go.
Another generation needed him,
Crying with their hunger,
their confusion,
burned blood.
It was then that he said to himself,
I shall be a witness for their age, too.

His second life began with a second trip to the Soviet Union. The Russia of 1926 had changed:

The change in ten years was remarkable . . . it was a nation sure of itself. . . . The folk were better dressed and food was much more plentiful. There were no unemployed and all the children were in school. . . . Here was a self-confident nation ready to fight for existence. The people of the nation did not have all they wanted or planned to have, but much more than ever before.

From Russia he went to China for the first time. Communism had not yet come to Imperial China. It would be thirteen years before Chairman Mao Tse-tung and his Communist party reigned supreme and established "the dictatorship of the working class."

In sharp contrast to his outlook on the Soviet Union, Du Bois was not pleased by the China of 1936. He was intensely disturbed by the presence of so many foreigners in the country and became even more distressed when he discovered that European businessmen controlled most of its capital, commerce, mines, and rivers. In fact on his first visit he had occasion to compare Shanghai with Mississippi, because the whites in China acted like the whites in the South.

When he arrived back at Atlanta University, Dr. Du Bois started his teaching of graduate students and updated his pioneering work in African studies. Moreover, using *The Communist Manifesto* as his text, he developed three courses on communism. Du Bois claimed that he had the best library of Marxist literature in the South: "I had not thought of propaganda. I was not and never had been a member of the Communist party. But I saw the growth of socialism and believed in the possibility of communism. I was convinced that no course of education could ignore this great movement."

America was also starting her new life. Her citizens had rejected the Republican administration of Herbert Hoover at the polls, and everyone was talking about a new day, a new deal which a man named Franklin D. Roosevelt was supposed to bring about.

President Roosevelt came into power with a bang. He greatly expanded the roles, functions, and activities of the federal government, making his office the guardian of the nation's welfare. FDR's programs for national reconstruction were designed to help labor and industry so that the collapsed wheels of the economy could start rolling again. Naturally there were those who objected to these trends, but FDR assured his critics that they had "nothing to fear but fear itself."

Afro-Americans stood to gain from the objectives of the New Deal—recovery, relief, reform. The programs were not designed specifically for blacks, but they made up three million of the eighteen million people on relief.

Du Bois watched America's recovery with critical eyes. He approved of and praised many of the new programs but was critical of the administration's go-slow policy on racial discrimination. In theory the federal government professed opposition to discrimination. But since many of the programs were in the hands of racist local officials, blacks benefited very little from theories in Washington.

The Depression years made a profound impact on Du Bois's social, political, and economic ideas. They made him aware of some of his own contradictions.

I was bitter at lynching, but not moved by the treatment of white miners in Colorado or Montana. I never sang the songs of Joe Hill, and the terrible strike at Lawrence, Massachusetts, did not stir me because I knew that factory strikers like these would not let a Negro work beside them or live in the same town. It was hard for me to outgrow this mental isolation, and to see that the plight of the white workers was fundamentally the same as that of the black, even if the white worker helped enslave the black.

No doubt these years confirmed Du Bois's belief in socialism. "When now the Depression came and thousands of workers, black and white, were starving . . . I began to awaken and to see in the socialism of the New Deal emancipation for all workers, and the labor problem, which included the Negro problem . . ."

Starting to resolve these inner political differences, Du Bois found more energy to devote to his work. Between 1934 and 1940 he published three important volumes: *Black Reconstruction in America, 1860–1880* (a history of black participation in the governments of the Southern states after the Civil War); *Black Folk, Then and Now* (a study of the black role in history); and *Dusk of Dawn* (an autobiographical account of his concept of the American race problem).

In 1940 he founded the journal *Phylon* in which he intended to publish articles on sociological research about blacks. In 1941 Du Bois became coordinator of a field-research program which Negro land-grant colleges helped to sponsor. It seemed for a while that the Atlanta studies he had started years ago would come alive again, but in the end most of the proposed projects failed. Nevertheless he must be regarded as the grandfather of the current student demands for black studies.

Then came the unexpected: Du Bois was invited to rejoin the staff of the NAACP. Ten years had passed; he had not followed its activities and therefore could not imagine what special service they wished him to perform. Nonetheless Du Bois accepted. He had retired from teaching, and the thought of being back on familiar turf fascinated him. He could not wait to see his old friends.

But it was not like coming home. Almost immediately the retired professor was aware of the enormous changes which the organization had undergone. "The results astonished me. The income had quadrupled, the membership approached a half million; the staff had tripled or more. It had become a big business, smoothly run and extraordinarily influential."

Du Bois did not approve of this Wall Street image but accepted it as an inevitable step on the part of the NAACP's desire to modernize and compete in a changing America. That he could understand. What left a bad feeling in his heart was that the organization had lost its most important feature, democracy. The give-and-take, back-and-forth discussion and debate were, as the Ghanaians say, "finish." Orders came down from on high and were expected to be performed efficiently, quickly—without questions.

Walter White was still in power and as before blocked many of the moves which Du Bois decided to make. Du Bois hesitate and remained cool. Finally he struck back. Within a matter of months he challenged White's dictatorial regime.

In 1945 the NAACP was invited by the United Nations organization to attend its meetings in San Francisco. The NAACP board selected the Barrington scholar to represent them, but Walter White, acting without board authorization, took the job himself and carried Du Bois along as his assistant. Both procedurally and in substance Du Bois found the San Francisco meeting disappointing. White made it difficult for Du Bois to carry out his propaganda in pursuance of civil rights for Africans. Du Bois felt that the UN was only superficially concerned about issues of racism and imperialism. He repeated some of the arguments which he had advanced early that year in his book *Color and Democracy: Colonies and Peace*, in which he accused the international mandate commission of its go-slow movement in awarding Africans self-determination and pointed out in beautiful prose that the proposed United Nations Security Council would be dominated by imperialist powers. His visit to beautiful northern California verified his earlier theories.

That fall W. E. B. Du Bois attended the Fifth Pan-African Congress in England. He was the grand old man of the hour, and in recognition of his lifetime devotion to African freedom he was elected president of the congress. It was a glorious event. A new generation of African leaders and intellectuals dominated the proceedings. They brought new and radical ideas to the body and told the world that African nationalism would free the continent of all remaining forms of imperialism. Among those present was an impressive young man called Kwame Nkrumah. People listened to his militant words. In seven years this beautiful man would be prime minister of a newly formed nation—Ghana.

It was during this time that Du Bois's wife died. Their marriage had lasted fifty-three years. Marriage to a man like Du Bois is probably not to be envied. From a distance, with his charm, degrees, and intelligence, he appears to be the greatest human being on earth. But living with a man with such extraordinary gifts could be a nightmare.

Du Bois does not tell us this about his marriage. Or does he? "It was not an absolutely ideal union, but it was happier than most, so far as I could perceive." Which is to say that anything bad which he might do would still turn out better than that which most people could do. "It suffered from the fundamental drawback of modern American marriage: a difference in aim and function between its partners; my wife and children were incidents of my main life work. I was not neglectful of my family; I furnished a good home. I educated the child and planned vacations and recreation. But my main work was out in the world and not at home."

In spite of everything Du Bois no doubt loved his wife very much up until the death of his son. After that little was left. "Our first born died—died not out of neglect but because of a city's careless sewage. His death tore our lives in two. I threw myself more completely into my work, while most reason for living left the soul of my wife. Another child, a girl, came later, but my wife never forgave God for the unhealable wound."

When his wife died he wrote: "My first marriage life lasted over a half century, and its ending was normal and sad, with the loneliness which is always the price of death."

Later Dr. Du Bois married a woman forty years younger than himself whose lifework was similar to his own. Du Bois said about her, "The faith of Shirley Graham in me was therefore inherited and received as a joy and not merely as a duty. She has made these days rich and rewarding."

Back on the political front Du Bois was again in a protracted struggle with the NAACP board. Over and over again he came into new conflicts with its establishment's conservatism. It strongly cautioned him against his radical involvement and asked him repeatedly to water down his explicitly pro-Soviet views. But as always Du Bois did what he wanted. Du Bois lasted for four years before he was fired. He never returned.

Writing about those years, Du Bois praises the NAACP for its early record and tells all blacks that they should be proud of that period. Du Bois, however, is strongly critical of the post-World War II NAACP because it never expanded its social philosophy and could therefore never organize the masses of blacks or restate their grievances at any meaningful level. Today young black critics both inside and outside the NAACP carry on Du Bois's fight against the executive board and are constantly seeking as did Du Bois to push it in the direction of radical reform. It is likely that with conservatism running wild in white America and radicalism pounding away in black America the NAACP will be forced to move more and more away from its middle-class orientation.

Here dead we lie because we did not choose
To live and shame the land from which we sprung.
Life to be sure is nothing much to lose
But young men think it is and we were young.

A. E. HOUSMAN

The Trial of Ideas

In 1948, determined to continue his agitation for social justice, W. E. B. Du Bois was offered and accepted the position of vice-chairman of the Council on African Affairs. This group was organized in 1939 by Max Yergan (a black YMCA secretary) and Paul Robeson (the famous black actor and singer). Four years later they were joined by Dr. Alphaeus Hunton, and the three of them, with the help of Frederick V. Field, a fine African-art collector, created a dynamic organization in New York. The group's functions ranged from raising funds for South African miners on strike to giving lectures on African history and culture throughout the country.

In the early 1950's the federal government stepped in. Through the Attorney-General's office the Council was placed on a list with other groups which were said to be subversive. By subversive the government meant any group it considered was working in some capacity for a foreign country whose object was to overthrow the United States government. The Communist witch-hunt scare which ensued sent a wave of fear through the Council. It created confusion and division, and many members resigned.

This was during the McCarthy era, a very ugly and frightening period in American history. The Soviet Union was now a world power, and many people in the United States seemed threatened by the thought that communism would take over the country. As in the New England of the past, Senator Joseph R. McCarthy's purges caused a frenzy of reaction. Communism was a magic word that set off and supposedly justified many abuses of justice. Trials were not necessary. The mere accusation implied one's guilt; long hair, the wrong friends, critical remarks about America, or reading the wrong books furnished the evidence.

Dr. Du Bois was a victim of this kind of hatred and political hysteria. He had worked for world peace for forty years and saw no justifiable reason why his present activities should be branded subversive. Like Paul Robeson he protested. The Council on African Affairs was not a Communist organization even though some of its members were. Du Bois felt that the council was doing a worthwhile job, and as long as it was a legal body he saw no reason why the government should interfere.

The United States government had its own ideas about what it could or could not do. Du Bois's political activities for the past ten years and his recent support of the cultural and political leaders of the Soviet Union convinced the Justice Department that Du Bois and his associates were secretly working for the Kremlin.

As we have seen, W. E. B. Du Bois had always been an outspoken and honest critic of American democracy. But after the war and the rise of the Soviet Union as a world power, there was a strong anti-Communist sentiment in the country. Every criticism was interpreted as a statement in support of Russia. Communism was not only a condemnation of America, but an alternative. Of course Du Bois left little for interpretation. He was the only one of twenty-five Americans who accepted, after the 1949 Paris Peace Congress, the offer to visit the Soviet Union. In a speech before one thousand persons he presented a well-organized attack on the American system. Du Bois told his audience that "American democracy fails to function." He said that the political and economic life was in the hands of the few: "They may be beneficial decisions, they may be detrimental, but in no case are they arrived at by democratic methods."

He went on to say:

The claim of the United States that it represents democracy in contrast to fascism or communism is patently false. . . . Today in the United States, organized wealth owns the press and chief news-gathering organs, and is exercising increased control over the schools and making public discussion and even free thinking difficult and often impossible.

The next statement caused officials in Washington to wonder: "The cure for this and the way to change the socially planned United States into a welfare state is for the American people to take over the control of the nation in industry as well as government. . . . If this be treason, make the most of it."

When he returned home, he continued his work for peace. He constantly held up the Soviet political experience as the future of civilized man. Since he could not find a liberal magazine which would publish his work, Du Bois published exclusively in far-left journals such as *New Africa, Masses & Mainstream*, and the *National Guardian*. He denounced the European Marshall Plan for economic recovery and was sternly opposed to rearmament. He also ran for public office on the American Labor party ticket but was miserably defeated. And to make a bad scene worse Du Bois accepted the chairmanship of the Peace Information Center (PIC), a flagrantly "subversive" group.

Uncle Sam would have no more. The Justice Department ordered the members of the PIC to register as agents of a foreign government. The eighty-two-year-old civil-righter refused, probably saying "How dare they." They dared even more. For refusing to register William Edward Burghardt Du Bois was indicted as a criminal under the Foreign Agents Registration Act.

The indictment alienated him from many of his friends because, as Du Bois said, "I found myself being punished before I was tried. . . . The Department of Justice allowed the impression to spread that my colleagues and I had in some way betrayed our country." Later he was to write:

Today in this country it is
becoming standard reaction
to call anything "communist"
and therefore subversive
and unpatriotic which
anybody for any reason
dislikes. We feel strongly
that this tactic has already
gone too far; that it
is not sufficient today
to trace a proposal
to a communist source
in order to dismiss it
with contempt.

But that was not enough to clear his face of the Red mud. Even after he was acquitted of the charges, many of his associates avoided him. In fact a dinner honoring his eighty-third birthday was almost canceled because many of the guest speakers, including Charlotte Hawkins Brown (president of Palmer Memorial Institute), refused to attend. Everyone was afraid. The hand of public scorn had pointed at Du Bois, and no one wanted to be branded along with him.

But E. Franklin Frazier, the chairman, stood firm and said the dinner must go on. It did at Small's Paradise, a black-owned Harlem club which welcomed Du Bois and his guests.

For the next ten years Du Bois went into a kind of semiretirement without losing his critical perspective. With some reservation he praised the Supreme Court school-desegregation decision of 1954 but denounced political leaders for doing "exactly nothing" to encourage the drive for integration. Professor Rudwick gives us an account of these years:

From the sidelines, during his last years, he avidly followed the work of the direct activists in their bus boycotts and lunch-counter sit-ins. While these demonstrations did not comprise a basic assault on the economic system, he was proud that the participants in the Montgomery boycott had been "the black workers."

Du Bois's interest in Africa and Asia also increased. The Chinese Communists were now in power, and the man called Kwame Nkrumah was slowly leading his West African state to independence.

In 1953 the World Peace Council awarded Du Bois a $7,000 peace prize, and later in the decade he received the coveted Lenin Peace Prize. But he could not travel because the United States government would not release his passport.

On Paul Robeson's sixtieth birthday W. E. B. Du Bois, now ninety, spoke out again in protest:

The persecution of Paul Robeson by the government and people of the United States during the last nine years has been one of the most contemptible happenings in modern history. Robeson has done nothing to hurt or defame this nation. He is, as all know, one of the most charming, charitable and loving of men. There is no person on earth who ever heard Robeson slander or even attack the land of his birth. Yet he had reason to despise America. He was a black man; the son of black folk whom Americans had stolen and enslaved. Even after his people's hard won and justly earned freedom, America made their lot as near a hell on earth as was possible. They discouraged, starved and insulted them. They sneered at helpless black children. Someone once said that the best punishment for Hitler would be to paint him black and send him to the United States. This was no joke. To struggle up as a black boy in America; to meet jeers and blows; to meet insult with silence and discrimination with a smile; to sit with fellow students who hated you and work and play for the honor of a college that disowned you—all this was America for Paul Robeson. Yet he fought the good fight; he was despised and rejected of men; a man of sorrows and acquainted with grief and we hid as it were our faces from him; he was despised and we esteemed him not.

Why? Why? Not because he attacked this country. Search Britain and France, the Soviet Union and Scandinavia for a word of his against America. What then was his crime? It was that while he did not rail at America he did praise the Soviet Union; and he did that because it treated him like a man and not like a dog; because he and his family for the first time in life were welcomed like human beings and he was honored as a great man. The children of Russia clung to him, the women kissed him; the workers greeted him; the state named mountains after him. He loved their homage. His eyes were filled with tears and his heart with thanks. Never before had he received such treatment. In America he was a "nigger"; in Britain he was tolerated; in France he was cheered; in the Soviet Union he was loved for the great artist that he is. He loved the Soviet Union in turn. He believed that every black man with blood in his veins would with him love the nation which first outlawed the color line.

I saw him when he voiced this. It was in Paris in 1949 at the greatest rally for world peace this world ever witnessed. Thousands of persons from all the world filled the Salle Playel from floor to rafters. Robeson hurried in, magnificent in height and breadth, weary from circling Europe with song. The audience rose to a man and the walls thundered. Robeson said that his people wanted Peace and "would never fight the Soviet Union." I joined with the thousands in wild acclaim.

This, for America, was his crime. He might hate anybody. He might join in murder around the world. But for him to declare that he loved the Soviet Union and would not join in war against it—that was the highest crime that the United States recognized. For that, they slandered Robeson; they tried to kill him at Peekskill; they prevented him from hiring halls in which to sing; they prevented him from travel and refused him a passport. His college, Rutgers, lied about him and dishonored him. And above all, his own people, American Negroes, joined in hounding one of their greatest artists—not all, but even men like Langston Hughes, who wrote of Negro musicians and deliberately omitted Robeson's name—Robeson who more than any living man has spread the pure Negro folk song over the civilized world. Yet has Paul Robeson kept his soul and stood his ground. Still he loves and honors the Soviet Union. Still he has hope for America. Still he asserts his faith in God. But we—what can we say or do; nothing but hang our heads in endless shame.

Finally in 1958 Du Bois was allowed to visit Europe.

August 8 was a day of warm and beautiful sunshine, and many friends with flowers and wine were at the dock to bid me and my wife goodbye. For the fifteenth time I was going abroad. I felt like a released prisoner, because since 1951 I had been refused a passport by my government on the excuse that it was not considered to be "to the best interest of the United States" that I go abroad. It assumed that if I did I would probably criticize the United States for its attitudes toward American Negroes. This was certainly true.

Dr. Du Bois and his wife Shirley remembered this trip with much happiness. Everything seemed perfect: the sea was calm throughout, the accommodations were excellent, and the other passengers were friendly. Du Bois was somewhat amused to discover that Americans traveling abroad could be so courteous. Du Bois loved the sea and spent most of his time reading, writing, and relaxing with his wife. Their first port of call was London, and Du Bois felt that his luggage was subjected to a more careful examination than he was accustomed to.

Using Paul Robeson's apartment as his base, Du Bois

trekked up and down the English countryside visiting old friends and his daughter, who was attending a secondary school near Bedales, outside London. For the ex-editor of *The Crisis* it was a glorious holiday.

That fall Du Bois made his fourth trip to the Soviet Union. He was given the grand tour. At Red Square in Moscow he celebrated with a half-million Russians on November 7, Independence Day, a famous holiday of the Russian state. From the Lamonosov State University Dr. Du Bois received an honorary doctorate in historical science.

While touring Russia he suddenly became ill and was rushed to a sanitarium: "I was weary from travel. . . . We had servants for every wish, and all were as kind as can be. I was there a month, and had every probe and test possible. My heart was measured a dozen times, my blood tested, my blood pressure taken, and I was poked inside and out."

After he recovered, upon his request, Du Bois was granted an audience with Prime Minister Nikita Khrushchev. For nearly two hours Du Bois and Shirley Graham discussed with him the American peace movement, Pan-Africanism, and the World Peace Council. Du Bois also told the head man in Russian politics the controversial story of his indictment and acquittal. Beyond that Du Bois wanted to discern the Soviet attitude toward African independence and proposed to the Soviet leader the idea of establishing an Institute of African Studies under the Russian Academy of Sciences.

African independence was no longer a dream because

Ghana, formerly the Gold Coast, had become independent from Great Britain a year earlier. Du Bois felt that the Soviet Union could be of great assistance to the rise of these new nation-states. "The scientific study of Africans and their continent was necessary for the guidance of their education and the organization of their culture. This was one of the ways in which the progressive world could help its lagging parts and one in which there were the fewest causes for friction and diversity of interest."

Dr. Du Bois wrote that this visit was one of the most important events in his life and made a profound impact on his thinking. Again and again over his five-month visit Dr. Du Bois was impressed with the Soviet achievement. He felt that the Communist party was helping to shape a new person and that this new person had a vested interest in whatever happened in Russia. In 1959 he wrote:

Across these squares yesterday a half-million people marched, walked, and danced; they ate and sang, they laughed and cheered. This morning when I arose and looked out, there was not a scrap of paper or sign of dirt. That meant work in the night I'm sure, but it meant much more than this: it meant that most of this half-million people dropped no dirt and threw away no paper, and they did this not under orders, but because they felt these squares were theirs, and they must not soil their own.

[What he saw] was more than triumph in physics; it was the growth of a nation's soul, the confidence of a great people in its plan and future. . . . The Soviet Union seems to me the only European country where people are not more or less taught and encouraged to despise and look down on some class, group or race. I know countries where race and color prejudice show only slight manifestations, but no white country where race and color prejudice seems so absolutely absent.

Defying the State Department, Du Bois left Moscow for China. He felt that the United States had no legal right to restrict his travel and "Certainly the United States could give me no less protection in China than it could in Mississippi." In eight exhausting weeks he traveled five thousand miles. By railway, boat, plane, car, and walking he saw the ancient cities of Peking, Shanghai, Hankow, Canton, Chungking, Chengtu, Junming, and Nanking. Du Bois traveled China's vast rivers, visited villages and communes, lectured at its colleges and universities, and met with Mao Tse-tung and Chou En-lai.

Although the doctor seemed more charmed by developments in Russia, he felt in one sense closer to the Chinese "because it is a land of colored people." Du Bois wrote:

I used to weep for American Negroes, as I saw what indignities and repressions and cruelties they had passed; but as I read Chinese history in these last months and had it explained to me stripped of Anglo-Saxon lies, I know that no depths of Negro slavery in America have plumbed such abysses as the Chinese have seen for 2,000 years and more. . . . Despite all this, China lives . . . Oh beautiful, patient, self-sacrificing China, despised and unforgettable, victorious and forgiving, crucified and risen from the dead.

Meantime the newly elected president of Ghana, Kwame Nkrumah, was calling the All-African conference. Du Bois was a little hurt but not surprised that he had not received a personal invitation from Nkrumah.

I sensed immediately that opposition had arisen in Africa over American Negro leadership of the African peoples. This had happened in 1920, when the West African Congress acknowledged no tie with the First Pan-African Congress in Paris which sparked it. American Negroes had too often assumed that their leadership in Africa was natural. With the rise of an educated group of Africans, this was increasingly unlikely.

Later, however, Du Bois received an invitation to the Ghana conference, but his Russian physicians advised him against such a taxing trip. His wife went instead. Shirley Du Bois, the only non-African to address the conference, read a message from her husband (see Appendix II).

William Du Bois cautioned Kwame Nkrumah, and by extention other African leaders, to beware of Greeks bearing gifts. He further warned the Ghanaian leader that experiments with private enterprise would retard the rapid growth of his economy. Du Bois felt that socialism was the future and offered it as the system best suited to the African personality and social conditions. Consistent with Du Bois's lifelong belief, he advised Nkrumah to push for Pan-Africanism, which

Du Bois hoped would ultimately lead to a federation of independent African states.

On Du Bois's ninety-first birthday, the Chinese honored him with a national celebration. Like the speech his wife presented in Accra (see Appendix II), Du Bois's Peking speech struck at American racism and extolled what he considered the virtues of the Soviet Union and China. Again, he warned Africans and Asians:

Beware Africa, America bargains for your soul. America would have you believe that they freed your grandchildren; that Afro-Americans are full American citizens, treated like equals, paid fair wages as workers, promoted for desert and free to learn and travel across the world.

This is not true. Some are near freedom; some approach equality with whites; some have achieved education; but the price for this has too often been slavery of mind, distortion of truth and oppression of our own people.

Tired but thoroughly pleased by this action abroad, the veteran of the civil-rights struggle returned home again. The witch-hunt hysteria had subsided, and the Old Man was surprised but again pleased not only by the welcome he received, both from friends and the government, but also because he was allowed to keep his passport. The United States Supreme Court ruled in the cases of Waldo Frank and William Worthy that the State Department had acted outside the scope of its constitutional authority in restricting the travel of Americans.

Now W. E. B. Du Bois prepared to die. He wrote,

"I am a little puzzled now about the ordering of my life. Several times in the past I find that I have prepared for death and death has not come." So as he had done at fifty and again at sixty Du Bois planned his weeks very carefully and avoided long-range commitments. "Always on my desk lies a calendar of my own devising with daily and hourly tasks; with plans for the week and next week . . . months are no longer absolutely mine. . . ."

But death did not come. Indeed a third life was soon to begin, for in October, 1961, several months before his ninety-fourth birthday, Du Bois joined the American Communist party and left the United States to spend his remaining years in Ghana.

Your face is the face I see in the market places
And in the fields,
You squeeze in beside me
In the tro-tro
And the lorries
On the bumpy road,
I can see now, why your heart needed this lovely
place.

LIZABETH GANT

The Du Bois I Knew

Blacks like me, mostly intellectuals and students with the left-wing involvement that characterizes those of my generation, did not understand why Du Bois had joined the Communist party at this late date. The Old Man from Great Barrington had been our spiritual and intellectual father, and his decision to join the Communists threw us into disarray. Frankly we disapproved of his actions and to some extent many of us felt that it would have a negative effect on the struggle of American black people for social equality.

We agreed that American society could not reform itself and that radical changes were needed in the basic institutions. We were becoming increasingly more enraged and embittered over the gradualist theory of social and political change in America. We deeply respected those brave blacks and whites who had started the sit-ins, stand-ins, and pray-ins, but we were also convinced that their doctrine of "nonviolent direct action" would ultimately have little political consequence on the white men who ruled in Washington. We had accepted James Baldwin's words "that the conscience of the South is the conscience of the nation" and did not therefore believe that the civil-rights movement in its present form was relevant. Integration? Well, for us it was a nightmare. We reasoned that integration into the existing American reality would be a combination of Negro inferiority, white liberal guilt, paternalism, and patronization, despite the righteousness of the civil-rights appeal.

Although we accepted communism as a condemnation of racism and capitalism, it was not our alternative. We did not believe the Russians either. We had listened to Marxist theories and had learned some important history lessons. But Marx was German and dead. And his workers of the world, already freed from their chains, were now too fat and rich to arise and do anything except read their insurance premiums. Beyond that, labor unions were among the most racist institutions in America. In principle we did not attack the Communists, but we felt that their promises of the good life were too distant, too foreign, and too dogmatic. Personally I was horrified by the thought of listening to Ray Charles in Russian.

What we wanted was a political, social, and cultural movement that would address itself to our peculiar racial history. But we saw nothing to identify with. For a while it was the Muslims, but that passed. We had lost faith in God, in our government, and in America. Most of us were looking to Africa for direction.

We learned that Du Bois had gone to Ghana. That pleased me because I was also en route to this West African nation, and if *The New York Times* was correct, I could look forward to seeing him soon. I felt that Du Bois owed us an explanation.

The Ghana of 1970 is not the Ghana that Du Bois saw. It still has the same topography, and the major ethnic groups are still Akan, Twi, Fanti, Ga, Ewe, and the Mashi-Dagamba group of Voltaic people. There are still fifty-six indigenous languages; its national flag is still a tricolor of red, yellow, and green horizontal stripes with a black star in the center of the yellow stripe.

The Ghana of 1961 was politically different. The first independent nation in West Africa has been ruled since 1969 by Dr. Kofi A. Busia. But that government has only been in power for a short while. From early 1966 to October, 1969, the country was ruled by a military body called the National Liberation Council. It came to power through a military coup and over-threw the civilian government, the Convention Peoples

Party (CPP), which had ruled the country under the leadership of Kwame Nkrumah without opposition for fourteen years. The differences in the two Ghanas is very important. It is unlikely that W. E. B. Du Bois could have functioned in the 1970 Ghana, in spite of its talk about democracy. Historically he belongs to the Ghana of Kwame Nkrumah.

Du Bois's Ghana had just emerged as an independent nation. For more than half a century the British government had ruled the country as a colony. The Ashanti of central Ghana had fought seven wars with the British to keep the territory free. But the British defeated the powerful military confederacy of the Ashanti and changed the course of Ghanaian history. After World War II, Ghana (which was called the Gold Coast until 1957) experienced political and constitutional advances on a scale equaled by few African countries. After the initial grant of a measure of self-government at the local level in 1942, African demands for independence led in 1949 to the appointment of an all-African committee to inquire into constitutional reforms.

Kwame Nkrumah was then the most powerful man on the scene. It is not too far from the truth to call him the Father of Ghana. His party, the CPP, took advantage of the constitutional reforms, agitated for more reform, struggled peaceably with the British for independence, and by 1961 was firmly in power. Like most politicians in the new nations of Africa, President Nkrumah had many friends and an equal number of enemies. He favored his friends with jobs and privileges and watched his foes from a safe distance.

From 1954 to 1961 Kwame Nkrumah steadily gained control over all aspects of Ghana's economic, political, cultural, and military affairs. His autocratic rule led to mounting but disorganized opposition.

Naturally Du Bois was in the friendly camp. He had known Nkrumah for twelve years and was pleased that he was leading the Ghanaian revolution.

When Ghana became independent in 1957, Du Bois, who was not then allowed to travel outside the United States, sought to advise Nkrumah by mail. He told Nkrumah that Ghana's achievements had pleased him greatly. Du Bois also told Nkrumah that he should work for peace "and join no military alliance and refuse to fight for settling European quarrels." He further advised the young president that Ghana should work for Pan-Africanism, socialism, and the welfare state. Du Bois ended his counsel with:

I pray you, my dear Mr. Nkrumah, to use all your power to put a Pan-Africa along these lines into working order at the earliest possible date. Seek to save the great cultural past of the Ashanti and Fanti peoples, not by inner division but by outer cultural and economic expansion toward the outmost bounds of the great African peoples, so that they may be free to live, grow, and expand; and to teach mankind what nonviolence and courtesy, literature and art, music and dancing can do for this greedy, selfish, and war-stricken world.

Du Bois had been invited by Nkrumah to found and

direct a secretariat for an *Encyclopaedia Africana* in Accra, the capital of Ghana. The *Encyclopaedia* was to be sponsored by the Ghana Academy of Sciences, and the Ghana government would underwrite the cost. The objectives of the secretariat were to plan and co-ordinate the work of assembling and publishing research which had an "authentic African viewpoint" and at the same time would be a product of scientific scholarship. Ghana was to be the headquarters, but all other African countries were to participate equally. Advice from eminent scholars in various African states had been sought. The editorial board included Africans from other states, and in due course funds for research and publication would come from other independent African nations. It was Du Bois's intention to draw on the skills of non-African scholars who had already advanced "accurate interpretation of African civilizations and cultures."

Favorable reactions had come from all over the world; and by 1962 after the formal launching of the *Encyclopaedia* at the University of Ghana, where Du Bois spoke, hard work began.

I arrived in Ghana early in 1963. In a newly independent nation the capital city is much like a gold-rush boomtown: confusion, noise, buildings going up and buildings coming down. Picture Accra: taxi drivers who forget to refill their gas tanks, Hausa-speaking traders in beautiful African robes selling maybe-shockproof watches; thousands of different kinds of people desperately hustling to make a living. Add to this, constant heat, the smell of red-hot-pepper food, and the laughter of an unpretentious humanity. Then you can imagine Accra.

Trying to see the Messiah would probably have been easier than seeing W. E. B. Du Bois. Beyond the impossible red tape there were two other formidable obstacles. First, there were the amazing but necessary security precautions. Person or persons unknown had tried to assassinate Nkrumah. Rumor had it that the United States CIA was trying to overthrow his government because of Ghana's militant anti-American policies. From friendly but unofficial sources I learned that it was believed in certain government circles that Afro-Americans had been involved in the attempted assassination conspiracy. And I saw several large posters which read: *"Beware of Afro-Americans."* Presumably no one thought that Du Bois was in any personal danger, but since Du Bois was in close contact with the president, anyone desiring to see Du Bois was immediately checked out.

The next barrier came as sort of a surprise. I was not considered important enough to see Du Bois. That is, I had no special rank, title, or revolutionary political credentials. As a Ghanaian lawyer using the pidgin English of his fellow-countrymen said, "Leslie, you don' be big man." In spite of the country's socialist leanings, class distinctions and *who you were* ran deep in the belly of the society. In Ghana, as elsewhere in the new nations of the world, class distinctions are more irritating, since differences between people are more noticeable. The rich are very rich; the poor are very poor. And there are few citizens in the middle class.

I accepted the security precautions. But they seemed strange in connection with Du Bois. When I had met him in America, I had almost collapsed with elation just shaking his strong hand. He had always been available, especially if a young black man needed to see him. In the fifties in America there was no need to protect him from meddlesome tourists or idlers. Like Paul Robeson he was avoided like the plague. People were afraid to go near him. Respectable Negroes avoided him because they did not want to be tarred and feathered with thick red Communist paint.

Finally I was given an audience. Dr. and Mrs. Du Bois lived in the Cantonment, where the senior civil servants, high-ranking government officials, chief political figures, and rich Europeans lived. Also, except for the Americans, Chinese, and Russians, who lived closer to the president's office, the Cantonment was the section of Accra where most foreign diplomats lived.

By African standards it was considered elegant. By American standards it would compare with a lower-middle-class neighborhood without any modern conveniences. The section was lovely with greenery and trafficless streets for the children to run in. Even before I talked to the Old Man I had seen him several times walking the lonely road which circled around and served each family in this quiet little area. On all those occasions he had his walking cane, a summer shirt with woolen pants, a light sweater tied around his waist, a book, and a pad. Every time I saw him he was with

Julian Mayfield, an Afro-American who was the editor-in-chief of the leading Ghanaian magazine, the *African Review,* and was said to be a special speechwriter for President Nkrumah. Whenever Du Bois saw me driving by, he smiled and nodded politely and continued his daily constitutional. I must confess that after seeing him the first time I planned my drive to coincide with the hour of Du Bois's stroll. This was easy since the scholar from Great Barrington was a slave to schedule and punctuality.

The homes of the Cantoment, built primarily for British colonial personnel around 1930, were simply constructed of rather cheap building material. Each family got approximately two bedrooms, a large combination living and dining room, usually a study, a bath—and four servants with their ever-increasing families who lived in a two-room bathless house about one hundred feet from the main house. To protect the big house and its smaller families from snakes, mosquitoes, moths, june-bugs, and other insects which buzzed and crawled around day or night, each was outfitted with porch screens and mosquito nets. No such precautions were taken for the hired help. Like most servants in Ghana as well as in most developing societies, the Cantoment servants were badly treated, overworked, and underpaid. The master—servant relationship had been inaugurated under the colonial system in which a small white minority had dominated a large black majority. Since independence little had been done to change this degrading colonial institution.

It was said to me that Dr. Du Bois did not want servants. Perhaps. But like a very few others in the country who could afford them (both Ghanaian and foreigners who felt that having them would be in conflict with their notions of the "people revolution"), he accepted his black help as part of the natural order of life. It was said that Du Bois's servants did only the bare minimum of domestic duties and spent most of their time studying educational courses that he had prepared for them. Beyond that he taught them other useful skills and unlike most other "masters" paid them a reasonable wage.

The evening we were scheduled to see Dr. Du Bois, I was very nervous, happy, weary, and generally confused. For days I had planned many questions to ask him. I had an early supper and at about six o'clock three of us—all Afro-Americans—drove from the University of Ghana at Legon to the Cantoment.

Du Bois's house, located near the center of the compound, was typical; I think it was a bit more elegant because of the green hedges which surrounded it. In front of the house were two policemen, and it was obvious from their uniforms that they had come from the Mashi-Dagamba ethnic group. They were tall and impressive, but the people in the capital regarded them as illiterate if not stupid. As one Ghanaian put it, "The tall men from the North do not think. They are trained to follow orders."

Prettier than the greenery and not from the same tribe as the Northerner was a beautiful woman sitting near Du Bois's porch. She was from the Ga tribe, the major ethnic group in the capital. She was probably the wife of one of the stewards, and at night women like this usually set up shop—a kind of bush department store —to sell such items as peanuts, cigarettes, bananas, oranges, kola nuts, and razor blades to the other servants in the Cantoment.

Then I saw W. E. B. Du Bois. My insides were heavy, but I managed to look quite normal when I shook his hand. Although I knew he wouldn't remember, I reminded him of our first meeting. He laughed. I laughed. And in that moment of remembrance I put my arms around his shoulders, squeezed in gently, and helped him back to his seat.

The living room looked and sounded like a small United Nations diplomatic lounge. All the major countries were represented, and I heard at least ten languages being spoken. We were introduced to everyone, and finally we took our seats near the smiling Chinese.

Dr. Du Bois did not look well. He coughed a few times, bringing silence to the room, and several times his body shook for no apparent reason. But for someone close to one hundred years old, he looked very good. I laughed silently because after sitting there for five minutes I forgot about all the questions I had wanted to ask him. So often that happens when the young are around the old.

He was a gracious host. He was interested in all his guests, and when he got around to me again, we had a long talk about peace in the world. The Old Man supported the efforts for peace but felt that the movement in the United States was too narrowly focused politically. That is to say he felt that Americans talked about peace in absolute terms. One could be for peace in Vietnam, he believed, but must support all the violent efforts of the South African freedom fighters. That led him into a discussion of his other views, and for nearly an hour he held us at absolute attention. His mind was clear; his words lucid. With tremendous honesty the Old Man reexamined many of his earlier political positions. He felt that he and Garvey had more in common than not, and that the latter had given great service to the cause of "oppressed people." He reviewed with amazing accuracy his relationship with the past leaders in the United States. Du Bois felt that he had learned much from Booker T. Washington but said that neither he nor Washington understood the nature of capitalistic exploitation of labor and the necessity of a direct attack on the principles of exploitation as the beginning of labor uplift.

The Old Man had become a Ghanaian citizen because he had lost faith in the United States. He felt that his ex-country had betrayed her claims to the justice of the American Revolution. He felt that life in the United States had become decadent and commercial; everything had been reduced to buying and selling. Du Bois accused the United States of being a war-mongering nation, a "supergovernment criminal wasting fantastic sums of money and lives on preparation for war." The Soviet Union, he believed, was the only nation that could now lead the world. After that statement the Chinese in the room stopped smiling. The Old Man went on to say that the Russians had developed a creative educational system, free of historical distortion. He supported his contention by citing the Sputnik program putting the Russians first in space. Although he was highly critical of the United States, Du Bois, like Thomas Wolfe, believed that it still had "magnificent possibilities" and was the "home of noble souls and generous people."

In closing he said that he was not sorry for having lived so long. He loved his work and felt that he had lived honestly with devotion to duty. He told us about his new autobiography and bade us good night.

Dr. Du Bois had not discussed his reasons for belatedly joining the Communist party, and for a number of reasons I had not been compelled to ask him about it. It did not seem important then. I felt very good driving back to Legon.

Several days later, while hundreds of Americans were marching on Washington, D.C., demanding political reform, William Edward Burghardt Du Bois died believing American society could not reform itself. A century was over. Du Bois was dead. A New Englander who became an African had died at the age of ninety-five. His black soul had come full circle, his history was complete: from Africa to Harvard and back to Africa.

When I
die
I'm sure
I will have a
Big Funeral . . .
Curiosity
seekers . . .
coming to see
if I
am really
Dead . . .
or just
trying to make
Trouble . . .

MARI E. EVANS

Let Us Cheer the
Lonesome Traveler

We knew of his illness, but we did not want to believe that Du Bois might die. We hoped he would live forever. The night before his funeral we held a wake and I planned final details about the funeral.

From early morning hundreds of curious souls entered the Cantoment to view the remains. The sun was warm but hearts were heavy. I watched the faces of the mourners. Even those who did not understand the historical significance of the moment were stricken with grief.

Du Bois's body lay in an open coffin, which had been placed inside a makeshift African hut. He was surrounded by all the traditional symbols which are always present at the burial of an African chief, but consistent with his politics he was dressed like a Chinese Communist leader.

Everyone passed the coffin quietly; all looked in; a few prayed; a Muslim leader chanted a prayer in Arabic; a Ghanaian woman put a flower on his chest; a few cried; most were silent.

I finally stood before him. I counted the lines in his face and recalled his smile of a few days past. I let my tears come freely; I touched him. I closed my eyes and thought of his book *The Souls of Black Folk* and realized that the old man lying before me was the Father of Soul, a brother man. The brothers' father; Father of the brother. A New Englander who became an African. From Africa to New England and back. He lived a hundred years without freedom. A century of protest. And before any of them, before Martin, Malcolm, Marcus, the man from Barrington, with all of his hang-ups and contradictions, had been scholarly, committed to freedom, violent, gentle and black—before any of them he was a black man, black people, and had come to Africa to die.

I passed by the coffin.

Even the cold war was relaxed as the Russians, Chinese, and Americans came to the same spot to pay their last respects. The United States representative was obscene and ugly. He was a Southern cracker who had come for political reasons, because the Russians were there and because the United States didn't want to be criticized in the Ghanaian press. Symbolically and actually his presence desecrated the meaning of the service. The Chinese and the Russian officials were doing their own political thing, but we black Americans were more concerned with the cracker.

Then, almost out of the heavens (security was good that day), I saw the President of Ghana, Osagyefo (Chief of Chiefs) Dr. Kwame Nkrumah, standing near his dead mentor. Kwame Nkrumah was a beautiful man. He looked like a president. And that's a special kind of look in a developing nation, for the man in that country must look like a lot of faces to a lot of different people. He must look poor and rich without appearing phony. He must be able to talk to the urban dwellers without offending the people of the land.

And now he was standing over William Du Bois, a man who had respected him, a man who thought that the president, whom Du Bois had called "my president," would unite Africa under one government and slowly create a Pan-Africana. Nkrumah stood there a long time, his body erect, motionless—watching the end of an era. I felt that in his mind he was saying, "Rest in peace, Black Soul. You were our beginnings before we were born, before oppression, without consciousness. There at Fisk or perhaps at Atlanta, you, my brother, my friend, my mentor—started what I will finish. You lived a long time and you saw other freedom fighters like Garvey, George Padmore, C. L. R. James, Wallace

Johnson, and so *many*, *many* others who never knew freedom, nor Africa, and in that they never knew life. Beautiful man, who came from so far to come home, I love you. How long you have struggled for our freedom. How long, brother, how long? How you must have suffered too. It will not have been in vain. We will continue until all black people are free. So take your rest. . . ."

And then with tears in his eyes the president, the man whom William Du Bois wanted to carry forth his tradition, reached into the casket and kissed the soul of Africa. I knew afterward, when the casket was closed and Brother Nkrumah led the body to the state funeral, that black men, unmistakably, had a glorious history.

Thousands of non-English-speaking Ghanaians lined the road as the body moved from the Cantoment to its final resting place. They were Africans, but only a few knew what was happening. It was a holiday, and death was in the air, and they would see the important men in the country. . . . The sun was hot like always but we had to move slowly to the beat of the drum, until finally we reached the burial site.

William Edward Burghardt Du Bois, born February 23, 1868, died August 27, 1963, was laid to final rest with full military honors on the afternoon of August 29 at a spot some fifty yards from the pounding ocean in a special grave next to his friend George Padmore, just outside the walls of a slave castle at Osu, residence of the ex-president of Ghana.

I felt strangely detached from the eulogies of the

funeral. They were not adequate, and the Methodist minister doing most of the Bible reading seemed like a contradiction in terms. I created in my mind the kind of funeral I would have given W. E. B. Du Bois. I would have had all the great poets (both living and dead) whom Du Bois had either known or respected pass the open coffin and read a few of their lines.

His old friend *James Weldon Johnson* would have been first in line. He would stand before the coffin a long time before he spoke. And then softly:

> Weep not, weep not,
> He is not dead;
> He's resting in the bosom of Jesus.
> He's borne the burden and heat of the day,
> He's labored long in my vineyard,
> And he's tired—
> He's weary—
> Go down, Death, and bring him to me.

And then a tall black man would appear. *Paul Laurence Dunbar*. He too was a special friend. He knew Du Bois long ago. His words are sad:

> Because I had loved so deeply,
>   Because I had loved so long,
> God in His great compassion
>   Gave me the gift of song.
>
> Because I have loved so vainly,
>   And sung with such faltering breath,

The Master, in infinite mercy,
 Offers the boon of death.

And then the beautiful *Claude McKay* would come from
the 1920's. He would want to read all his poetry but gives
us only a little:

 I would go back to darkness and to peace,
 But the great western world holds me in fee,
 And I may never hope for full release
 While to its alien gods I bend my knee.
 Something in me is lost, forever lost . . .

Melvin B. Tolson? Yes. He was a friend too.

  One more river to cross
  Oh, how can we forget
  Our human rights denied
  Our manhood crucified.

Richard Wright:

  I am nobody
  A red sinking autumn sun
  Took my name away.

  Make up your mind snail!
  You are half inside your house
  And halfway out!

  In the falling snow
  A laughing boy holds out his palms
  Until they are white . . .

Margaret Walker would place a rose on his chest. She is

sad of course but smiles a little because it is her first trip to
Africa. She reads from her poem "For My People":

> Let a new earth rise
> Let another world be born.
> Let a bloody peace be written in the sky.
> Let a second generation full of courage
> issue forth, let a people loving freedom
> come to growth, let a beauty full of
> healing and a strength of final clenching
> be the pulsing in our spirit and our blood.
> Let the martial songs be written,
> let the dirges disappear.
> Let a race of men now rise and take control.

Countee Cullen:

> What is Africa to me
> Copper sun or scarlet sea.
> Strong bronzed men, or regal black
> Women from whose loins I sprang
> When the birds of Eden sang?
> One three centuries removed
> From the scenes his fathers loved,
> Spicy grove, cinnamon tree,
> What is Africa to me?

Then *Langston Hughes* with tears in his eyes would end
the first group of readings:

> I've known rivers:
> I've known rivers ancient as the world
>   and older than the flow of human blood
>   in human veins.

My soul has grown deep like the rivers.
I bathed in the Euphrates when dawns were young.
I built my hut near the Congo and it lulled me to sleep.
I looked upon the Nile and raised the pyramids above it.
I've known rivers:
Ancient, dusky rivers.
My soul has grown deep like the rivers.

Then would come the African poets. The first would be
Leopold Sedar Senghor from Senegal:

New York! I say to New York, let the black blood
flow into your blood
Cleaning the rust from your steel articulations,
like an oil of life
Giving your bridges the curve of the hills,
the liana's suppleness. . . .
And the ears, above all the ears to God
who with a burst of saxophone
    laughter created the heavens and the earth in six days.
And on the seventh day, he slept his great negro sleep.

And then *Jean-Joseph Rabearivelo* from Madagascar:

        The black glassmaker
        whose countless eyeballs none has ever seen,
        who is strong as Atlas
        and who carries the seven skies on his head.

And *David Diop* also from Senegal:

        In your presence I rediscovered my name
        My name that was hidden under the pain of
            separation

I rediscovered the eyes no longer veiled
   with fever
And your laughter like a flame piercing
   the shadows
Has revealed Africa to me beyond the
   snows of yesterday.
And in your presence I have rediscovered
   the memory of my blood
And necklaces of laughter hung around
   our days
Days sparkling with ever new joys.

My fantasy was over, and the preacher man was still saying his amens after each sentence. He spoke about everything except those ideas and values which W. E. B. Du Bois had lived for. He was making ready the Old Man's soul for God; whitewashing a newly acquired Ghanaian spirit.

If only I had shouted: Preacher man, brother man, minister of God! You do not know the man who lies in state beneath you. He comes from another country, another time, another century. He was born in America. New England: By a golden river in the shadow of two great hills. His skin was darker than the other boys'. He knew that he was unique. He was black, and they were of English and Dutch descent, and some were of a large migration of Irish and German workers who tended the mills. He was poor too. But he was proud, mingled with the upper classes, shared their beliefs and destiny, their ideas of property and their illusions. But reality had the last word. He wanted to go to Harvard, the "greatest and best" but had to go South instead. It took Fisk, years of looking at black, brown, and yellow beauties, years of violence and America's inability to be rational to make young Willie see that every lynching was a blow to his own manhood.

After the death of Frederick Douglass, black people prayed for another leader to deliver them. Douglass had done much, but much work remained. They had listened well at their Sunday go-to-meeting preachings and hymnings; they had worshiped long the creed of an unseen God, "washing ironing cooking scrubbing sewing mending hoeing plowing digging planting pruning patching dragging along never gaining never reaping never knowing and never understand . . ."

After Fisk, he went to Harvard. For his people he needed the best education. But Harvard had a serious fault: racial discrimination. Yet he would survive. He wanted only a first-class education and avoided situations which he thought would embarrass him. After Harvard, there was Germany, a place Du Bois loved so much. He felt that Europeans related to him and not his color. In *Dusk of Dawn* he wrote, "Europe modified profoundly my outlook on life and my thoughts and feelings toward it."

From Europe he brought back the beginnings of an ideological system. W. E. B. Du Bois believed that the Afro-American could only prosper through self-development and through the goodwill of whites. Du Bois believed that only black could lead black, and the leaders had to be well educated and sensitive. This leadership, the black avant-garde, was called the Talented Tenth. Although Du Bois did not seem to ever advocate total separation as a solution to racism, he was also strongly opposed to complete assimilation. He wanted to see cultural differences among people preserved. What Du Bois wanted was to give his race a sense of its own self-consciousness.

From the fall of 1894 to the spring of 1910 Du Bois was a teacher. As he wrote, "I was going to study the facts, concerning the American Negro and his plight. . . . The decade and a half in which I taught was riotous with the happenings in the world of social development, with economic expansion, with political control, with racial difficulties." Out of this came a body of research and theories of social and political change. He was one of the first to start research on Africa and did a great deal to strike a hard blow to European racial notions about Africa.

Then came Booker T. Washington. Du Bois opposed him because he considered Mr. Washington a conciliationist par excellence. Du Bois did not understand the full significance of Washington's appeal. Washington did soft pedal civil rights, but as far back as 1900 he counseled Afro-Americans to seek self-determination through economic sufficiency. And after 1940, Du Bois changed his mind. He felt that the NAACP was too narrowly focused, and he counseled blacks to establish their economic cooperative commonwealth in America.

After Washington's death, William Du Bois moved to the center of black protest. The Harvard-trained Du Bois had to admit that the Hampton-trained Washington had done a great deal at Tuskegee to promote industrial training and economic growth. But the Tuskegeean had failed to understand the complex relationship between power politics and economics and minimized the importance of higher education. As Professor Elliot M. Rudwick said, "The Tuskegeean did not allow the establishment of a division of labor—marking off for each group a particular type of program and emphasis. Understandably he could not speak consistently on behalf of suffrage, higher education and social equality; but was it necessary for him to work against those who did?"

Then came Garvey. Du Bois came into open conflict with him. In a way Garvey had the best of both men, but like Du Bois was ahead of his time. He gave thousands of lost black souls a sense of pride and hope for a better future. But Garvey failed. Not so much because of government interference or not even because his talents as an administrator did not correspond to his propagandistic skills. Afro society had changed. The philosophy of integration was a powerful gospel. Afros wanted *in* not *out*. American blacks as a result of occupational differentiation, urbanization, and increased education had acquired wide-reaching interests.

After Garvey had been deported, Du Bois continued

the struggle and realized much later the power of Garvey's program. After the Depression and into the forties, Du Bois had come to the position that social justice was not possible in the present system. He embraced completely the doctrines of socialism and struggled in the NAACP for its control. But he was bound to fail. He was working against the history of the era. Many serious black intellectuals still believed that the system could be reformed.

Du Bois sought refuge in the far left. Until he left America, he was somewhat tragic. The government hounded him constantly; the "Negro race" turned its back on him, and the Communists used him. So, frustrated, old, and alienated, he joined the American Communist party, an almost inexplicable act for a man who had spent thirty years rejecting them.

But that did not worry us because we knew that Du Bois was primarily striking back at the country in which he was born. America had never recognized his greatness or his honor. Yet the world he created glows with undying life, and the ears of black men still listen to his words, his anger, his love for his people, and his lasting faith in the dignity of all men.

The funeral was over.

That evening, Dr. Kwame Nkrumah delivered the following message to the nation:

We mourn the death of Dr. William Edward Burghardt Du Bois, a great son of Africa.

Dr. Du Bois, in a long life-span of ninety-five years, achieved distinction as a poet, historian, and sociologist. He was an undaunted fighter for the emancipation of colonial and oppressed people and pursued this objective throughout his life.

The fields of literature and science were enriched by his profound and searching scholarship, brilliant literary talent, and keen and penetrating mind. The essential quality of Dr. Du Bois's life and achievement can be summed up in a single phrase: "intellectual honesty and integrity."

Dr. Du Bois was a distinguished figure in the pioneering days of the Pan-African movement in the Western world. He was the secretary of the first Pan-African Congress held in London in 1900. In 1919 he organized another Pan-African Congress in Paris which coincided with the Paris Peace Conference. When George Padmore and I organized the Fifth Pan-African Congress in 1945 at Manchester, we invited Dr. Du Bois, then already seventy-seven years of age, to chair that congress. I knew him in the United States and even spoke on the same platform with him. It was however at this conference in Manchester that I was drawn closely to him. Since then he has been a real friend and father to me.

Dr. Du Bois was a lifelong fighter against all forms of racial inequality, discrimination, and injustice. He helped to establish the National Association for the Advancement of Colored People and was first editor of its fighting organ, *The Crisis*. Concerning the struggle for the improvement of the status of the Negro in America, he once said:

"We will not be satisfied to take one jot or tittle less than our full manhood rights. We claim for ourselves every single right that belongs to a freeborn American: political, civil, and social; and until we get these rights, we will never cease to protest and assail the ears of America. The battle we wage is not for ourselves alone, but for all true Americans."

It was the late George Padmore who described Dr. Du Bois as the greatest scholar the Negro race has produced, and one who always upheld the right of Africans to govern themselves.

I asked Dr. Du Bois to come to Ghana to pass the evening of his life with us and also to spend his remaining years in compiling an *Encyclopaedia Africana*, a project which is part of his whole intellectual life.

We mourn his death. May he live in our memory not only as a distinguished scholar but as a great African patriot. Dr. Du Bois is a phenomenon. May he rest in peace.

And then we have William Edward Burghardt Du Bois's last words to the world. His last message was dated June 26, 1957. He had given it to his wife, Shirley Graham Du Bois, for safekeeping until his death.

It is much more difficult in theory than actually to say the last good-bye to one's loved ones and friends and to all the familiar things in this life.

I am going to take a long, deep, and endless sleep. This is not a punishment but a privilege to which I have looked forward for years.

I have loved my work, I have loved people and my play, but always I have been uplifted by the thought that what I have done well will live long and justify my life; that what I have done ill or never finished can now be handed on to others for endless days to be finished, perhaps better than I could have done.

And that peace will be my applause.

One thing alone I charge you. As you live, believe in life!

Always human beings will live and progress to greater, broader, and fuller life.

The only possible death is to lose belief in this truth simply because the great end comes slowly, because time is long.

Good-bye.

APPENDIX I

Du Bois's Final Statement on Communism, 1959.

I have studied socialism and communism long and carefully in lands where they are practiced and in conversation with their adherents, and with wide reading. I now state my conclusion frankly and clearly: I believe in communism. I mean by communism, a planned way of life in the production of wealth and work designed for building a state whose object is the highest welfare of its people and not merely the profit of a part. I believe that all men should be employed according to their ability and that wealth and services should be distributed according to need. Once I thought that these ends could be attained under capitalism, means of production privately owned, and used in accord with free individual initiative. After earnest observation I now believe that private ownership of capital and free enterprise are leading the world to disaster. I do not believe that so-called "people's capitalism" has in the United States or anywhere replaced the ills of private capitalism and shown an answer to socialism. The corporation is but the legal mask behind which the individual owner of wealth hides. Democratic government in the United States has almost ceased to function. A fourth of the adults are disfranchised, half the legal voters do not go to the polls. We are ruled by those who control wealth and who by that power buy or coerce public opinion.

I resent the charge that communism is a conspiracy: Communists often conspire as do capitalists. But it is false that all Communists are criminals and that communism speaks and exists mainly by means of force and fraud. I shall therefore hereafter help the triumph of communism in every honest way that I can: without deceit or hurt; and in any way possible, without war; and with goodwill to all men of all colors, classes and creeds. If, because of this belief and such action, I become the victim of attack and calumny, I will react in the way that seems to me best for the world in which I live and which I have tried earnestly to serve. I know well that the triumph of communism will be a slow and difficult task, involving mistakes of every sort. It will call for progressive change in human nature and a better type of manhood than is common today. I believe this possible, or otherwise we will continue to lie, steal and kill as we are doing today.

Message from W. E. B. Du Bois to the All-African Congress. Delivered by Shirley Graham Du Bois. 1958.

My only role in this meeting is one of advice from one who has lived long, who has studied Africa and has seen the modern world. I had hoped to deliver this word in person, but this was not possible. I have therefore asked my wife, Shirley Graham, to read it to you. It is simple and direct. In this great crisis of the world's history, when standing on the highest peaks of human accomplishment we look forward to Peace and backward to War; when we look up to Heaven and down to Hell, let us mince no words. We face triumph or tragedy without alternative. Africa, ancient Africa has been called by the world and has lifted up her hands! Which way shall Africa go? First, I would emphasize the fact that today Africa has no choice between private Capitalism and Socialism. The whole world, including Capitalist countries, is moving toward Socialism, inevitably, inexorably. You can choose between blocs of military alliance, you can choose between groups of political union, you cannot choose between Socialism and Private Capitalism, because Private ownership of capital is doomed.

But what is Socialism? It is disciplined economy and political organization in which the first duty of a citizen is to serve the state; and the state is not a selected aristocracy, or a group of self-seeking oligarchs who have seized wealth and power. No! The mass of workers with hand and brain are the ones whose collective destiny is the chief object of all effort. Gradually, every state is coming to this concept of its aim. The great Communist states like the Soviet Union and China have surrendered completely to this idea. The Scandinavian states have yielded partially; Britain has yielded in some respects, France in part and even the United States adopted the New Deal which was largely socialistic, even though today further American Socialism is held at bay by 60 great groups of corporations who control individual capitalists and the trade-union leaders.

On the other hand, the African tribe, whence all of you sprung, was communistic in its very beginnings. No tribesman was free. All were servants of the tribe of whom the chief was father and voice. Read of the West Coast trade as described by [J. E.] Casely-Hayford: There is small trace of private enterprise or individual initiative. It was the tribe which carried on trade through individuals, and the chief was mouthpiece of the common will.

Here then, my Brothers, you face your great decision:

Will you for temporary advantage—for automobiles, refrigerators and Paris gowns—spend your income in paying interest on borrowed funds, or will you sacrifice present comfort and the chance to shine before your neighbors in order to educate your children, develop such industry as best serves the great mass of people and makes your country strong in ability, self-support and self-defense? Such union of effort for strength calls for sacrifice and self-denial, while the capital offered you at high price by the colonial powers like France, Britain, Holland, Belgium and the United States, will prolong fatal colonial imperialism, from which you have suffered slavery, serfdom and colonialism. You are not helpless. You are the buyers of capital goods, and to continue existence as sellers of capital, the great nations, former owners of the world, must sell or face bankruptcy. You are not compelled to buy all they offer now. You can wait. You can starve a while longer rather than sell your great heritage for a mess of western capitalistic pottage.

You cannot only beat down the price of capital as offered by the united and monopolized western private capitalists, but at last today you can compare their offers with those of socialist countries like the Soviet Union and China, which with infinite sacrifice and pouring out of blood and tears, are at last able to offer weak nations needed capital on better terms than the West. The supply which socialist nations can at present spare is small as compared with that of the bloated monopolies of the West, but it is large and rapidly growing. Its acceptance involves no bonds which a free Africa may not safely assume. It certainly does not involve slavery and colonial control which is the price which the West has demanded, and still demands. Today she offers a compromise, but one of which you must beware: She offers to let some of your smarter and less scrupulous leaders become fellow capitalists with the white exploiters, if in turn they induce the nation's masses to pay the awful cost. This has happened in the West Indies and in South America. This may yet happen in the Middle East and Eastern Asia. Strive against it with every fibre of your bodies and souls. A body of local private capitalists, even if they are black, can never free Africa; they will simply sell it into new slavery to old masters overseas.

As I have said, this is a call for sacrifice. Great Goethe sang, "*Entbehren sollst du, sollst entbehren*"—"Thou shalt forego, shalt do without." If Africa unites it will be because each part, each nation, each tribe gives up a part of its heritage for the good of the whole. That is what union means; that is what Pan-Africa means: When the child is born into the tribe the price of his growing up is to give over a part of his freedom to the tribe. This he soon learns or dies. When the tribe becomes a union of tribes, the individual tribe surrenders some part of its freedom to the paramount tribe.

When the nation arises, the constituent tribes, clans and groups must each yield power and much freedom to the demands of the nation or the nation dies before it is born. Your local tribal, much-loved languages must yield to the few world tongues which serve the largest numbers of people and promote understanding and world literature.

This is the great dilemma which faces Africa today; faces

one and all: Give up individual rights for the needs of the nation; give up tribal independence for the needs of Mother Africa. Forget nothing but set everything in its rightful place: the Glory of the six Ashanti Wars against Britain; the wisdom of the Fanti Confederation; the unity of Nigeria; the song of the Songhay and Hausa; the rebellion of the Mahdi and the hands of Ethiopia; the greatness of the Basuto and the fighting of Chaka; the revenge of Mutessa, and many other happenings and men; but above all—Africa, Mother of Men. Your nearest friends and neighbors are the colored people of China and India, the rest of Asia, the Middle East and the sea isles, once close bound to the heart of Africa and now long severed by the greed of Europe. Your bond is no mere color of skin but the deeper experience of wage slavery and contempt.

So too, your bond with the white world is closest to those like the Union of Soviet Socialist Republics, who support and defend China and help the slaves of Tibet and India, and not those who exploit the Middle East, the West Indies, and South America.

Awake, awake, put on thy strength, O Zion; reject the meekness of missionaries who teach neither love nor brotherhood, but emphasize the virtues of private profit from capital, stolen from your land and labor. Africa awake, put on the beautiful robes of Pan-African Socialism.

> You have nothing to lose but your Chains!
> You have a continent to regain!
> You have freedom and human dignity to attain!

For Further Reading

Abrahams, Peter, *Tell Freedom*. New York, Alfred A. Knopf, 1954.

Adams, Julius J., *The Challenge: A Study in Negro Leadership*. New York, W. Malliet, 1949.

Aptheker, Herbert, "The Washington-Du Bois Conference of 1904." *Science and Society*, 13:344–51 (Fall 1949).

Brisbane, Robert H., "The Rise of Protest Movements Among Negroes Since 1900." Unpublished doctoral thesis, Harvard University, 1949.

Broderick, Francis, "W. E. B. Du Bois: The Trial of His Ideas." Unpublished doctoral thesis, Harvard University, 1955.

Chesnutt, Helen M., *Charles W. Chesnutt, Pioneer of the Color Line*. Chapel Hill, University of North Carolina Press, 1952.

Cox, Oliver C., *Caste, Class and Race*. Garden City, Doubleday, 1948.

Cronon, Edmund D., *Black Moses*. Madison, University of Wisconsin Press, 1955.

Franklin, John Hope, *From Slavery to Freedom*. New York, Alfred A. Knopf, 1948.

Garvey, Amy-Jacques (ed.), *Philosophy and Opinions of Marcus Garvey*, 2 vols. New York, Universal Publishing House, 1923–25.

Locke, Alain, *The New Negro*. New York, Albert & Charles Boni, 1925.

Logan, Rayford, *What the Negro Wants*. Chapel Hill, University of North Carolina Press, 1944.

———, *The Negro in American Life and Thought*, 1877–1901. New York, The Dial Press, 1954.

Padmore, George (ed.), *History of the Pan-African Congress.* Manchester, 1945.

————, *Pan-Africanism or Communism.* New York, Roy Publishers, 1956.

Record, Wilson, *The Negro and the Communist Party.* Chapel Hill, University of North Carolina Press, 1951.

Redding, J. Saunders, "Portrait of W. E. Burghardt Du Bois." *American Scholar*, 18:93–96 (Winter 1948–49).

Rose, Arnold M., *The Negro's Morale.* Minneapolis, University of Minnesota Press, 1949.

Terrell, Mary Church, *A Colored Woman in a White World.* Washington, Ransdell, Inc., 1940.

Washington, Booker T., *Up From Slavery.* Garden City, Doubleday, 1900.

Books by W. E. B. Du Bois

Du Bois's published works are extensive: eighteen books, more than twenty long pamphlets, hundreds of editorials in *The Crisis* and *Horizon*, many articles in Negro newspapers, and an even larger number of articles in scholarly journals.

1. *The Suppression of the African Slave Trade to the United States of America, 1638–1870.* Harvard Historical Series, No. 1. New York, Longmans, Green, 1896; New York, Russell, 1965. 355 pages.
This book, Du Bois's Ph.D. thesis at Harvard University, is considered one of the best studies on the importation of Africans to the New World.

2. *The Philadelphia Negro: Together with a special report on domestic service.* Series in Political Economy and Public Law, XLV. Philadelphia, University of Pennsylvania, 1899. 520 pages.
A sociological study of the black community in Philadelphia. It is an excellent study, probably Du Bois's best.

3. *The Souls of Black Folk: Essay and Sketches.* Chicago, A. C. McClurg, 1903; New York, Fawcett Publications, 1964. 264 pages.
An account of Du Bois's racial and political attitudes, written in fiery and beautiful prose. James Weldon Johnson stated that the book had "a greater effect upon and within the Negro race than any other single book published in this country since *Uncle Tom's Cabin.*"

4. *John Brown.* American Crisis Biographies. Philadelphia, George W. Jacobs, 1909. 406 pages. Revised edition with new preface and conclusion by author, New York, International Publishers, 1962. 414 pages.
The story of the white abolitionist who led an interracial band

of men against the slave system at Harper's Ferry. It is probably Du Bois's flimsiest work, lacking the historical analysis and understanding found in his other books.

5. *Quest of the Silver Fleece.* Chicago, A. C. McClurg, 1911. 434 pages.
Du Bois began working on this novel at the turn of the century; it is a fictionalized statement of his views on the black problem. When it appeared in 1911, very few people read it. Nevertheless, this book gave Du Bois a chance to write about a wide variety of black problems. It is a love story involving Blessed Alwyn and Zora, the daughter of a black conjurer. The action begins in an Alabama school run by a Wellesley graduate, but before the wedding day we are exposed to every conceivable problem of the times: white society, machinations in the Republican party, and lynching. Then we witness exploits of the schoolmarm's Northern industrial family in their dealings with black workers. But before the story ends, Bles and Zora are married, presumably to live happily ever after. Du Bois described this book in his autobiography as "really an economic study of some merit."

6. *The Negro.* Home University Library of Modern Knowledge, XCI. New York, Holt, Rinehart & Winston, 1915. 254 pages.
A restatement of some of his earlier views, with very little new information. As Frederick L. Broderick said in *W. E. B. Du Bois: Negro Leader in a Time of Crisis*, "nothing which indicates the mind or hand of an original scholar."

7. *Darkwater: Voices From Within the Veil*, New York, Harcourt, Brace & World, 1920. 276 pages.
Here Du Bois traces his life and accomplishments from his boyhood in Great Barrington. He is sharply critical of white America, and his literary style is rather sardonic.

8. *Dark Princess: A Romance*. New York, Harcourt, Brace & World, 1928. 311 pages.

Appearing almost a decade after the beginning of the so-called Negro renaissance, it did not have the literary excitement of his first novel. Unable to enroll in a necessary course in obstetrics for racial reasons, an Afro-American medical student, Matthew Towns, is forced to leave New York University. In Europe, Towns becomes involved with an international conspiracy of black elites seeking to replace the dominant worldwide white group. His work for the conspiracy leads Towns into all kinds of intrigues and jobs and finally to jail when he attempts to kill some Ku Klux Klan members. For the most part, the characters are static spokesmen for particular points of view, and Du Bois constantly displays his intellectual breadth with irrelevant references to Croce, Proust, Picasso.

9. *Black Reconstruction in America, 1860–1880*. New York, Harcourt, Brace & World, 1935; Cleveland, Meridian, 1962. 746 pages.

An admirable work. Supported by grants from the Rosenwald Fund and the Carnegie Foundation, it was a model of Du Bois's work as a scholar. At the core of the book were his defense of Reconstruction governments and his economic interpretation of the North's desertion of the Negro. Considered one of his most important and enduring works.

10. *Black Folk, Then and Now: An Essay in the History and Sociology of the Negro Race*. New York, Holt, Rinehart & Winston, 1939. 401 pages.

This work is primarily a rebuttal in anticipation of misrepresentations by whites during a time of rising American curiosity about the Negro. Du Bois felt that the kernel of this historical treatment of Negroes was a body "of fairly well-ascertained truth."

11. *Dusk of Dawn: An Essay toward an Autobiography of a*

Race Concept. New York, Harcourt, Brace & World, 1940. 334 pages.
A review of his life, decade by decade, which identifies the general black race problem with his own development. Du Bois's life is placed in a setting of world history.

12. *Encyclopedia of the Negro: Preparatory Volume with Reference Lists and Reports* (with Guy B. Johnson), New York, Phelps-Stokes Fund, 1945. 208 pages.
A historical chronicle which attempts to outline black contributions to world culture.

13. *Color and Democracy: Colonies and Peace*. New York, Harcourt, Brace & World, 1945. 143 pages.
A timely book which expresses Du Bois's hope for world peace. He reemphasizes his belief that colonial peoples must receive a share of power in the world if future wars between rulers and subject peoples are to be avoided.

14. *The World and Africa: An Inquiry into the part which Africa has played in world history*. New York, Viking, 1947. 276 pages. Enlarged edition, with new writings by the author from 1955 to 1961, New York, International Publishers, 1965. 364 pages.
In this classic review of African history, Du Bois documents the historic injustices of the rape of Africa from the slave trade to its partition by the Colonial powers. But he does this against a background of the vast contributions of ancient and modern Africa to world culture, industry, and peace.

15. *In Battle for Peace: The Story of My 83rd Birthday* (with additional comment by Shirley Graham). New York, Masses & Mainstream, 1952. 192 pages.
He refines his theories of race relations and outlines his views on world peace.

16. *The Black Flame*, Vol. I, *The Ordeal of Mansart;* Vol. II, *Mansart Builds a School;* Vol. III, *Worlds of Color.* New York, Mainstream, 1957, 1959, 1961. 316 pages, 367 pages, 349 pages. An extended fictional work interpreting Negro history from Reconstruction to the present. Like Du Bois's other novels this trilogy is neither a literary success or as valuable as his scholarly works.

17. *An ABC of Color: Selections from over a Half Century of the Writings of W. E. B. Du Bois.* Berlin, Seven Seas, 1963. 214 pages.
The selection was made by Du Bois; the book appeared shortly before his death.

18. *The Autobiography of W. E. B. Du Bois: A Soliloquy on Viewing My Life from the Last Decade of its First Century.* New York, International Publishers, 1968. 423 pages.
A unique personal commentary upon a century in which Du Bois played a consequential role. Written in his ninetieth year, the *Autobiography* is an account of a lifetime devoted to Afro-American liberation, rich in information and interpretation.

Major Articles by Du Bois

1. "The Enforcement of the Slave-trade Laws." *Annual Report of the American Historical Association*, 1891. Senate Misc. Doc. 173, 52nd Cong., 1st Sess. Washington, 1892, pp. 161–74.

2. "Results of Ten Tuskegee Conferences." *Harper's Weekly*, 45:641–45 (June 22, 1901).

3. "The Black North." *New York Times Magazine*, November 17, 24, December 1, 8, 15, 1901. (A series of five articles, two

dealing with New York City, one article each on Philadelphia and Boston, and a final article, "Some conclusions.")

4. "Of the Training of Black Men." *Atlantic Monthly*, 90: 289–97 (September, 1902).

5. "The Talented Tenth," in Booker T. Washington, *et al.*, *The Negro Problem* (New York, James Pott Co., 1903), pp. 31–75.

6. "The Training of Negroes for Social Power." *Outlook*, 75:409–14 (Oct. 17, 1903).

7. "The Negro Farmer," in *Negroes in the United States*. Bulletin No. 8, Bureau of the Census, Department of Commerce and Labor (Washington, D.C., 1904), pp. 69–98.

8. "The Niagara Movement." *Voice of the Negro*. 2:619–22 (September, 1905).

9. "The Economic Revolution in the South" and "Religion in the South," in *The Negro in the South: His Economic Progress in Relation to His Moral and Religious Development* (Philadelphia, 1907), pp. 79–122; 125–91.

10. "Socialism and the Negro Problem." *New Review*, 1:138–41 (February 1, 1913).

11. "Of the Culture of White Folk." *Journal of Race Development*, 7:434–47 (April, 1917).

12. "Marcus Garvey." *The Crisis*, 21:58–60 (December, 1920).

13. "Communists and the Color Line." *The Crisis*, 38:315 (September, 1931).

14. "Marxism and the Negro Problem." *The Crisis*, 40:103–04, 118 (May, 1933).

15. "Negroes and the Crisis of Capitalism in the U.S." *Monthly Review*, 4:178–85 (April, 1950).

Index

"... tremendously moving ... explains the depth of the black man's current resentment ..."

TO BE A SLAVE
by Julius Lester

Runner-up for the Newbery Medal, TO BE A SLAVE is a collection of the memories of ex-slaves, ranging in subject matter from capture in Africa to plantation life; from early resistance to life after emancipation. Presenting many aspects of the black man's experience in America which have previously been ignored or sugarcoated, TO BE A SLAVE contains some material never before published and some that has been extracted from sources long out of print. Mr. Lester has interspersed the actual words of slaves with his own commentary on the social and historical conditions of the times.

"This is how it was—a powerful chronicle of tragedy skillfully assembled from the eloquent slaves themselves, accompanied by pointed but unobtrusive editorial commentary and starkly dramatic illustrations."

—Best Books of the Year
School Library Journal

A LAUREL-LEAF BOOK 75c

If you cannot obtain copies of this title from your local bookseller, just send the price (plus 15c per copy for handling and postage) to Dell Books, Post Office Box 1000, Pinebrook, N. J. 07058. No postage or handling charge is required on any order of five or more books.

For everyone who wants to
understand the most crucial
issue in America today . . .

BLACK STRUGGLE

A Short History of
the Negro in America
by Bryan Fulks

The Black American's battle for freedom today has its
roots in centuries of injustice. BLACK STRUGGLE
recounts the history of the Negro from his early beginnings in Africa up to the headline-making events
of today. While it is a chronicle of suffering the cruelties of slavery, the humiliation of segregation, and the
imprisonment of urban ghettos, it is also a story of
heroism: the daring exploits of black soldiers, the
determination of slaves in revolt, the bravery of the
underground railroad escapes and the courage of the
civil rights martyrs.

A LAUREL-LEAF BOOK   75c

The Search for
Freedom and a New Life
in America . . .

The Outnumbered

Stories, Essays, and Poems About Minority
Groups by America's Leading Writers

Edited by Charlotte Brooks

An anthology about minorities of yesteryear, many of
whom are now assimilated, and minorities of today,
for whom the promise of America has not been ful-
filled.

A LAUREL-LEAF BOOK 60c